JUST A PEDLAR OF PILLS

by

Geoffrey S Knowles

Best wishes
Geoff
Aug 2009

Acknowledgements

I would like to thank my wife Colleen for all the help and encouragement in preparing this book. Her patience with my computer shortcomings greatly added to the final presentation.

My thanks to Ron Burke for designing the front cover.

I would also like to thank all those whose association with me has contributed to a variable and interesting journey through my life to date; without them there is no story.

First Published 2009 by Appin Press, an imprint of Countyvise Limited.
14 Appin Road, Birkenhead, CH41 9HH

British Library Cataloguing in Publication Data.
A catalogue record for this book is available from the British Library.

ISBN 978 1 906205 35 5

Pills

At eight o'clock each morning I take a little pill,
The first of many that I take to cure my every ill.
My second one, at 10 o'clock, that leaves me feeling righteous,
That's one designed to halt the onset of acute arthritis.
A pill to keep my blood pressure from soaring through the roof,
Another one for breathing, that's needed, that's the truth.
A pill to help my memory from failing all the time,
I must remember that one – to miss would be a crime.
I've pills for constipation, don't laugh, it isn't funny,
And pills to bung me up again if things get very runny.
Pills to add the vitamins it seems that I am lacking,
Capsules of Cod liver oil to keep my joints from cracking.
I've pills for this and pills for that, some are taken nightly,
With all the pills I daily take I should be feeling sprightly.
To regiment them all day is quite a daunting task,
But since I am a pensioner, I get them all for free,
But my BEST MEDICINE still remains –
my lovely CUP OF TEA

Contents

The Beginning	1
The Dark Clouds are Gathering	28
HMS King Alfred and Beyond	41
64th MTB Flotilla	55
A Moment in Time	63
Moving On	78
Further Progress	85
Victory in Europe	99
Minesweeping in the Far East	109
Singapore and Beyond	117
Back Home	128
Boom Town	141
Early Days at Hoylake	152
Moving On Again	160
The Seventies	169
The Revolution in the Pricing of Prescriptions	180
Getting Things in Perspective	190
Hospitals and Health	198
The Widening Scene	205
Hoylake Cottage Hospital	213
Wirral Postgraduate Medical Centre	222
The Statutory Committee of the RPSGB	230
Millennium	238
Epilogue	249
Curriculum Vitae	253
Letters	255

CHAPTER ONE

The Beginning

A Child is a person who is going to carry on what you have started. He is going to sit there where you are sitting and when you are gone attend to those things which you think are important. You may adopt all the policies you please, but how they are carried out depends on him. He will assume control of all your cities, states and nations. He is going to move in and take over your churches, schools Universities and Corporations. All your books are going to be judged, praised or condemned by him. The fate of humanity is in his hands.

- Abraham Lincoln 1861

To call upon the memory to re-enact events of over eighty years ago has resulted in my sitting down and just trying to recall so much of what is now a world past .Whether the past was good, or even better, can only be a trick of the mind, so that the advent of sentimentality will have to be excused. Others have done it before and so I might be excused if I do it from time to time.

Thus on the 10th December 1919 I came into this World in a small terraced house in Queensferry near Chester. My father James Ernest Knowles was at that time employed at the new Summers Steel Works at Shotton alongside the river Dee on the Welsh side of the border. Summers Steelworks had moved in 1910 from Ashton-under-Lyne where the original Company had been well known as Nail Makers. My father had started as office boy at the age of 14 years when his father died, and had progressed in his work so that at the later stages he was entitled the "Cashier" and became a principal signatory for documents and payments. It was a strange title and today he would be called the Accountant, which was borne out when he retired and was replaced by two Accountants!

I feel I never met my paternal Grandfather and my Grandmother but perhaps maybe only once. There was a Sister Ethel, two younger Brothers Albert and Joseph. Albert died at the age of thirteen when boarding at Warehousemen and Clerks School at Cheadlehulme and my Father was only informed of his death at school assembly the next day.

My "uncle Joe" was a frequent weekend visitor to our home, and this was not always appreciated by my mother, who after one of his returns from a Mediterranean Cruise (he was a bachelor then) brought back a present of a wicker footstool to which my Mother remarked at a later date "Must have been made in Birmingham." My father's Sister Ethel was not a frequent visitor, but her husband Harry Read spent a holiday with us from time to time. When I was very young, he would take me for a walk (a long way to me) to the Groves, which were down by the river Dee, and I remember him most because he always wore an overcoat and brown knitted woolen gloves. The Groves were also a popular place to go on Sunday evenings in the summer because there was always a Band Concert held in the Bandstand. My father always enjoyed these concerts and always took me with him.

My mother, who was ten years younger than my father, came from Trefnant in North Wales where my Grandfather (Taid) owned a not over successful brickworks and in addition contrived to have a family of eight children, all living in a home built corrugated-iron House. Whatever his failings as a brickworks owner, he was in addition a professional joiner. He managed to produce a family of two boys, four girls, then two boys, all of whom I was privileged to know over many years; and whose diversity of occupation and interests were fascinating. The eldest one called John Oliver Edwards was an expert practical engineer with the British Thompson Huston works in Wolverhampton and during the 1939-45 War he was of such importance that he was taken to work each day by taxi paid for by the company which was quite unusual for a man employed on the 'Shop Floor'. I do not remember the size of his family but I do recall that he had a son who became a manservant to an important man in the United States. The next son, my Uncle Llewellyn, was employed as a clerk in the Brymbo Steelworks, which was, located just outside Wrexham. I remember being taken for a walk by him when I was staying there and on passing a shop asked me if I wanted any sweets. I rapidly agreed with the suggestion and he then said *"Well have you got any brass then?"* which rather surprised me but it was much later that I appreciated this illustration of how little were his earnings in work in those days, and how they had to be carefully used. During the difficult mid thirties, the Steelworks was closed down and my Uncle became one of the many country-wide unemployed, but not to be outdone he immediately applied for a low-grade clerk's job at Williams and Williams Steel Windows establishment in Chester. I always remember that he came for his lunch to our house bringing with him a small suitcase containing his sandwiches and his toothbrush for he had some brand new dentures, the latter being new and costly so needed to be carefully treated. Just before the start of the War, he applied for, and was appointed the Office Manager to the Denbighshire Agricultural College. He loved this work and went to live in a small village just outside Denbigh. He and Maud, his wife, had one son called Roger now retired and with whom I make contact each Christmas.

The four daughters were called Nora, Marian, Ceridwen (my mother) and Gwladys, all of whom lived very active, interesting and busy lives. I did not know much about my Aunt Nora, except that she was married twice and had three children by her first marriage, Eleri, Diana (Dodie) and a son called Winston who was the eldest. As I remember Winston he had a shoe repairing shop on the side of Aunt Nora's second home in Harwarden, but when he was nineteen he elected to go to Australia and become a Priest in the Church of Australia. With my cousin Dorothy I sat on a bench in the Church Hall in Queensferry and listened to the speeches made in anticipation of his departure. At the conclusion a deep bass singer present elected to sing, and the song had a first line which began *"Many brave Souls lie asleep in the deep, So Beware – Beeee-ware".* As Winston was about to board a ship (there were no aeroplanes then) and be on board for three weeks this seemed to me to be hilarious—and I still feel the same when I recall the occasion. Cousin Eleri was much older than me and she became a great friend and companion of my Mother after my father died. Dodie married a reporter and spent many years in South Africa and returned home when her husband retired. It always amused me that Aunt Nora's second husband was called Sam Weigh, which I thought was a very appropriate name for a "coalman"!

Aunt Marian who was a very strict formidable character but wonderfully kind, had a huge and powerful husband John Roberts whom she sent to Canada for three years to make some money before she would marry him. For many years, they owned the village store and butchers at Rhewl and I always marvelled at his strength that he was able to carry carcasses and cut them up for selling all on his own. He also had an enormous appetite and watching him devour a rice pudding in those old enamel tin dishes was quite forbidding, and I always thought that I should get at least two spoonfuls of it, but alas it was not to be. When I went to stay with them he always managed to take me to Rhyl for a swim in the open air baths and he was always in trouble when we got back for although he always denied our trip, she always knew where we had been. My aunt always saw that good use was made of me when I stayed with them for I was always detailed off to get on the delivery bicycle and make journeys with groceries to far distant houses. I wasn't always over excited about this unfair (in my opinion) use of my limited talents in this kind of work, but there was no escape. In later years they moved to Denbigh where he owned a small farm and where they spent the rest of their days. When my Uncle Jack died my son John and I represented the Knowles Family at the funeral and we sat in a chapel for over two hours listening to various worthies extolling the life of John Roberts and it was all spoken in Welsh! In deference to my son and I, the English language came momentarily to the fore with the words **"He was a Good man"**, at intervals of about twenty minutes and that was all the both of us understood. When my Aunt Marian died, amongst other gifts, she had left a small legacy to her four Nephews, but there was a stipulation that the four of us were to carry her coffin from the hearse to the grave the other side of Rhewl churchyard. This seemed to present no difficulty and by seniority my brother Alun and I were the pair at the front part of the coffin. Nothing went wrong except that Iris (Alan's Wife) ran alongside us exclaiming *"Alun can't do this he's got a Hernia"*. Whilst being very amusing it caused a little embarrassment and I still wonder how Alun felt, but as usual he was silent and said nothing. Towards the end of the war my aunt and uncle suffered the tragedy of Dewi, their nephew, being killed just at the bottom of the lane leading from the farm. I cannot imagine a more heartrending blow it must have been to them as he was temporarily in their care.

The third sister in the family was my mother Ceridwen, mostly abbreviated to Ceri. Her early life found her as an apprentice to a costumier and dressmaker in Ruthin and in addition she became very adept at Jacobean and Italian drawn thread embroidery and in later life was a much sought after teacher in the latter subjects, throughout Cheshire and North Wales. A number of these beautiful time-consuming works are now to be seen in various rooms in my home. Whereas people now sit and watch television, she would always be found sitting doing her embroidery no matter what else might be going on. She wasn't bad at darning socks either: a craft that now seems to be extinct! As a mother she was very industrious in the home, she had to be with two growing sons, and yet she found time to indulge in many extra mural activities. Amongst these was the Upton Women's Institute, the Chester Townswomen's Guild and also for a time she was a very active member of the King's School Mothers Guild. My brother Alun was certainly the apple in her eye and could do no wrong, whilst I always seemed to be considered rather dull and stupid, and many times I had the feeling that she thought her second born should have been a girl. But I wasn't! I always appeared to come in second. Early in my life she christened me "pepper pot" on account of my high spirits and easily roused temper, perhaps indeed my auburn hair (with some red in it) bore this out. This nickname continued

all through my childhood and I hated it. Perhaps this appears a little unfair and I know she loved me but this strange feeling has stayed with me all my life. Perhaps the worst illustration of what perhaps was her tactlessness was when I returned home on leave three weeks after D-day all she seemed to be concerned about was "Poor Alun" who served most of the War in Jerusalem doing a clerical job with the RASC! I would, however, add that just before she died I was the one who collected her from her flat to take her to the Nursing Home and on arrival, though very ill she said, *"I knew YOU would come for me."* Some questions in life are never answered.

All the family were very musical and their talents were used in many spheres. Every family has to have some 'skeletons' and my Aunt Gladys seemed to fit this title. When she was in her early twenties she married a Robert Kyffin, who after the wedding set off to Australia to make arrangements for her to follow him. Days went by, years passed, and he was never heard of again. He left behind a pregnant wife and in the fullness of time she gave birth to a daughter who was named Dorothy. After many years, he was legally presumed dead and Aunt Gwladys then married again to Dai Roberts, a rather pompous headmaster. I was never happy with the way he treated his stepdaughter, or me at times, but she survived and though now deceased herself had two husbands (not at the same time) and two daughters who were always very kind to her. The remaining two brothers, Bryn and Caradoc, completed the picture of a very active family. Bryn when aged only sixteen enlisted in the Army during the Great War. Many times he told Alun and I lurid tales of life in the trenches, some of which I now realize could only have been somewhat intentionally exaggerated. He came back a very broken man and never really came to terms with life. His ebullient humour and devilish expressions will always remain with me and perhaps it is a matter of regret that we saw too little of him. Caradoc the youngest was highly intelligent, in fact a genius, and at the tender age of fourteen passed his School Certificate whilst still at the village school in Trefnant. He went on to become a Heating Engineer. He married whilst quite young and this proved unfortunate and later broke up and he left her. He later found happiness and went to live with another lady whose name I cannot remember. They had a son called Dewi, even as bright as his father had been, but he was unfortunately killed in a road accident at a very young age, as I have mentioned before. Caradoc died at the age of thirty-four whilst working in Belgium where he contracted blood poisoning from which he never recovered; it was said he never really wanted to recover. He had caught an infection which took hold of him; modern medicine would have saved him, but sadly at that time there was no such help available The family however was very kind to his 'Widow' and it was unfortunate that the son Dewi was killed on the road just outside the farm whilst in the care of his Aunt Marian and her husband Uncle Jack at Denbigh.

However, I digress, the Knowles family had a historical pattern of clerical and financial occupations, but recent family research has found that some three generations ago one of my father's family was a druggist, which I mention, as until then I appeared to be the only one who had abandoned the family trait to become a pharmacist. Let me add at this time and make it plain a Chemist and Druggist, which was the title when I qualified, was not what we now know as a Drug Dealer! (If such people existed in the bad old days.) My father was a fair, but strict, disciplinarian and my brother and I were brought up to abide by this. The standard he set for us was the one he had set for himself, as he had been obliged to be the breadwinner at his home from the age of fourteen. He led a very quiet life, loved his home, and seemed to have little outside interests, except his unending and enduring support for Chester Football Club. I always thought that his early death after his retirement was the result of this pattern of just sitting at home and doing little other than go for walks and read books, but that was his choice, and that was his idea of leisure which he so well deserved after giving all his energies, and more, to looking after his mother and brothers and then bringing up his own family and serving his employers well beyond the call of duties, throughout the strains of two long Wars. He really was one of the last of a generation from the industrial towns in the north west who retired to the seaside, found no real friends there, and just faded away after a few years.

When I was about two years old (how would I know!) we moved from Queensferry to a quiet middle class terraced row of houses rejoicing in the name of "Melville" 24 Newry Park, Chester. I believe that my father made this move to be quite sure his sons should have the opportunity of a good education; which then resulted in him sending us both to the Kings School, Chester where the benefits of this decision were to help us both as we progressed in the days and years to come. The only person not really mentioned up to now is my brother Alun. Let's face it we were as different as chalk and cheese. But although we did not appear to be outwardly loving brothers there was a very deep bond which was always there and lasted throughout our lives even though life took us in very different directions at school, during our war service, and afterwards. After the war, he returned to the bank, made quiet progress and apart from his interest in playing cricket his energies were principally looking after the finances of Ellesmere Port Rotary Club. Alun was always a quiet person though he had a great sense of humour which was not always appreciated and certainly not by his French teacher at Kings School who wrote on his report at the end of one term, *"His Abysmal silence drives me to distraction!!"* He really could get under people's skin. He was married just after the war to Iris Parry, and a few hours before the wedding my son John, now aged about six, contrived to hide the wedding ring, but it was happily recovered in time for the event. It would appear they had a very happy, if isolated, life and having no children seemed to find it difficult to take adequate interest in the varied life of my two boys. I think this was unfortunate and I could never understand their total lack of interest and understanding of what were after all Alun's only two nephews. They both hardly endeared themselves to Jean when, for many years,they sent as a Christmas present to John and Peter a 5 shilling (50 pence) voucher each to cash at Browns of Chester which was mainly a ladies and mens clothing shop.

I do not think this was done any other than with the best thoughts in mind, but somehow that was how they saw things. In his late sixties Alun suffered poor health and I saw much more of him, including daily visits when he was in hospital for a long time. When he came home I went over to his house in Little Sutton on Saturday afternoons and, sitting in a little room upstairs, (why there I never knew) we both watched the Saturday sports on television and spent many happy hours reminiscing about days past, and of course Chester Football Club. He was only 72 when he died and in a strange kind of way I missed my big brother, even though life seemed to have prevented us seeing more of each other. Perhaps I was the one who understood his silences and perhaps knew more about how he ticked. and knew he was highly loved and respected in Ellesmere Port Rotary Club to whom he gave so many hours as treasurer and editor of the Talking Book they produced to those who needed and could benefit from this production. I never understood why he hid his talents all through his life and adopted this strange attitude of hiding his intelligence and not sharing his thoughts, as it always seemed too much trouble to push himself forward, and yet somehow I know inwardly that was not true, because he really was a true reflection of his father's qualities.

As mentioned before, my first memory of my life was at the age of two, sitting and being nursed on my mother's knee in front of a blazing fire from the kitchen range, (you may or may not remember the great big iron ovens, which had to be black-leaded each week.) It appears that at that time I was very poorly with an illness, not really heard of now, called Croup. However, I came through and proceeded to grow up in a normal happy contented home. As mentioned previously it was during these early years that I acquired the nickname of "pepper pot" which I hated and more so because my mother and Alun continuously baited me in the hope that I would explode in anger. As I approached my sixth Birthday, it was arranged that I should attend a Preparatory School in Hoole, which is on the outskirts to Chester. To get there I was able to travel by bus from the end of the road and walk back home a mile when school was over; I was only six years old! I can clearly remember that morning bus ride which went through country roads which now have all altered having been overtaken by housing development. The other memory was that the Crosville Bus had solid rubber tyres which made the journey quite uncomfortable. The walk back was along very quiet streets and took about half an hour. Once a year one of those streets, or roads, was closed for 24 hours as it was an undeveloped road and if this was not observed the road would cease to be a private one. This I understood was an ancient law and I sometimes wonder if this pertains today, but I doubt it very much. It was however interesting to see the Watchman sitting in a little wooden hut keeping himself warm with a brazier of glowing coals in front of him and I doubt there are such people as this today. This little difficulty once a year meant an even longer way home for a very little boy. A Mrs. Payne and her sister ran the school in a house with a very large front room, and we progressed in life by learning to write, chiefly by repetitive lines and lines of 'pot hooks' or similar strange letters. But it was also an exercise in learning how to get on with other children and I remember that I became very friendly with a little girl, surely this could not be part of the curriculum for coping with the future, or was it? After I had been there a few months and was walking home with one of my fellow pupils (not the little girl!), a cat ran out from a house we were passing and ran across the main road and I followed it without giving it a thought as to the danger. The next thing I knew was that I was on the ground the other side of the road hard up against a sandstone wall. Apparently, my thoughtless crossing had involved contact with two cars. Cars were very thin on the ground in 1926. It would appear that neither had collided with each other but I had been struck by one of them and now reposed with two badly torn knees. The car driver took me home to what must have been a very distressed mother; I cannot imagine how the driver of the car must have felt. A visit to the doctors revealed two badly cut knees and a mark down my spine, which it was concluded had been made by the mudguards of the car. This was a very close encounter with what could have been a disastrous injury. After convalescence and a lot of quite unwarranted sympathy I recovered and no permanent damage was left.

Whilst I was still at this school, an incident took place which was to have a profound effect on me all through my life. It appears that my father decided to take a half day off and take us to a place I had never heard of before called New Brighton. I was told we were going to the seaside, and I will not say I was disappointed when we got there, but there was an incident, which stands out more in my memory than the visit. During this visit we went for a trip on the Seacombe Ferry which sailed up and down the Mersey and whilst on the ship my father lifted me up and sat me on the stern rail. I was absolutely terrified and even today can see the swirling waters made by the propellers as they came out from the rear of the ship. This has left me with a fear of heights, which sadly remains with me to this day and has blighted my life over many years. I never sought to blame my Father but for such a thoughtful and careful man this has seemed so out of context. Parents of all kinds can make many errors in bringing up children; after all, there is no Instruction Book.

When I was seven years old, I became eligible to join the Kings School Junior School which was called Arnold House and was situated about a mile from the City Centre. My Brother Alun was already there and to confirm this advance I was bought a Kings School tie, one of those knitted ones which I hated, but which in more recent years became the things to wear by the hoi poloi in the Carnaby Street age in the Seventies! So armed with my new tie I went to Arnold House, which also contained a few Boarders in the same building. Thus began a three year stint in which I moved up a form each year. I well recall an arithmetic exam in the second year, when on returning home my father asked me how I had fared. My reply was confident and affirmative, only to be dashed when the results showed I had achieved only five marks out of two hundred and fifty! Across the road from the school was a playing field and at the end an area of gardens. Each boy was allocated a patch for a year and under instruction learned the rudiments of gardening and the development of plants from seeds. I doubt this happens now, for we now have quite a different approach to early education For Christmas in that year, which was my eighth, I had asked to be given "The Wonder Book of the Navy" which I read time after time and a little later I announced that I wanted to join the Navy but I didn't want to go to war. This was a source of much amusement at home. Events were to prove different many years later for on page 43 there were two pictures of one of our latest aircraft carriers named HMS *Furious* which took my interest, but little did I realize that not only would I go to war in the Navy but also I became a member of the crew of that carrier! A very strange twist in fate.

In the third year we were taught the elements of French using a phonetic system of sounds for pronunciation before the normal letters were used. This also reminds me that on one occasion when I was staying with my Aunt Marian in Rhewl she asked me if I could speak any Welsh, to which I replied in the negative but adding I was learning French; this caused those present much amusement, and her action both hurt my dignity and perhaps my egoism.

It was during this third year that an event happened which although long forgotten still haunts me. It was said that one or two of the older boys had been up to some mischief, the nature of which I never discovered, but it was of such disgrace that the leader was to be given a public caning. The whole of the Junior School were ordered to the gymnasium and on the stage was the headmaster, the boy, and two teachers. After a brief statement by the headmaster, none of which I understood or even remember, the boy was held over a chair by the two teachers and the headmaster proceeded to give the boy six strokes of the cane. After each one, the screams of pain were deafening and it was hard to believe it was happening. This was my first introduction to Public School customs, and at the time I felt it was an act of cruelty that would not even be considered or allowed some sixty years later. When I reached home, I was unable to eat my lunch as I disgorged this story to my mother. Whilst at Arnold House I made friends with one of the boys, a friendship which was later to touch me throughout my life. Arnold Jones was about a year older than me and did not move with me to the Upper School as his parents sent him to a Boarding School elsewhere. Later on when I was starting to learn botany at night school in Chester Museum at the beginning of my pharmacy apprenticeship who should turn up at the same classes but Arnold, who at that time was apprenticed to a Chemist in Ellesmere Port. He never went on to qualify, possibly because he was one year older and was caught up in the months before the start of the war and his early call up with the Cheshire Yeomanry. Then again when I opened my pharmacy in Ellesmere Port shortly after the war who should be the first representative to call upon me but Arnold Jones. Our two families became very close for a number of years as John and his children, Nat and Angela, grew up together, Angela later becoming Godmother to Peter. We also shared interests as fellow Masons, though my sojourn in Masonry was very short lived as I lost interest when I moved to Hoylake, possibly because I was too occupied with the pharmacy and growing sailing interests.

When I was eleven years old I moved to the Senior School, which was situated in the Market Square of Chester on the opposite side of the Town Hall. In more recent years, and certainly after my time, the lovely old sandstone School building adjoining the Cathedral was sold to Barclays Bank and the proceeds were invested in a new building situated about three miles out of Chester. I felt rather sad about this but later realized that the future of the school depended on such an arrangement taking place; as the old building would probably have been condemned if major expensive work had not had been carried out. In the Autumn of 1931 I found myself in the Form entitled Remove A, in those days the B Form was for the brighter children, and I could not understand why if my brother had been in remove B I should not be. This troubled me for some time, but I suppose the reason should have been obvious! But this produced an unfortunate result for me as in the next year I progressed to Form 3 Minus, the A and B having now been changed to Plus and Minus for some reason. I then finished as Top of the class at the end of that year and this brought promotion to Four Plus for the next year. This proved to be a bad decision, as I never flourished in the Plus Form and at the end of that year, I was held back for an extra year, eventually moving into the Upper Fifth, the School Certificate year, still struggling a little to attain the standard required.

What happened then was one of those things that have puzzled me ever since, for half way through the year I left School without ever having tried or taken my School Certificate Examinations which were due to be taken at the end of the Summer Term. What puzzled me more was what had come into my father's head, after all he had arranged so methodically, and then allow me to leave without any qualification that could be of help in the future.

Before I left school I had featured in the only school outside Liverpool that had ever won the Liverpool Schoolboys Shield, which we did so on a rainy afternoon on Everton

Football Ground. Afterwards we had to go to Liverpool Collegiate School to collect the Trophy, as they had been so confident of winning! Along with Trevor Owen, a fellow pupil, I had been selected to play for Chester School boys football team, and the arrival to this team by two boys from the "posh" school quite upset the other players at first. However we soon became part of the team and in that year Chester Schoolboys reached the semi-final of the English Schools Shield. Following this I was approached by Chester Football Club and selected to play in the A Team, and from time to time in the Reserve side and twice, but only twice, in the first team. The start of the war brought this to an end and I never played for them on my return six years later. Quite honestly I would never have made the first team as I was far too lightly built for that rough and tumble. Still it was an experience and who knows what might have happened? Another pleasant memory was being part of the school swimming team going to the Warehousemen and Clerks Boarding School in Cheadle Hulme, which as I mentioned earlier, was the boarding school my father and his brother had attended until the premature death of their father had necessitated my father having to leave and work to keep the family. In addition to my swimming I did quite a bit of rowing with the school. In those days we were not quite as proficient as Chester Kings School are now for it is only in later years that they have featured annually in Henley Regatta and similar events.

I had indicated to the Careers Master that I was thinking of becoming a pharmacist and he promptly produced leaflets for me but they were on farming as a Career! Perhaps he suffered with deafness, or was it just stupidity, or had he never heard of pharmacy, needless to say I was both annoyed as well as feeling it hideously amusing. There came a moment when I was in the fifth form, when an advertisement appeared in the local paper entered by a David Miln the proprietor of Miln's Seeds, requiring pupil apprentices. Possibly because of a conversation with my Father and being possibly persuaded, the net result was I left school in January 1936 and so came to work at Miln's Seeds. This change of direction of his career prospects for me was so unlike him, and he then paid out what I considered the massive sum of two hundred and fifty pounds to apprentice me to this seed firm in Chester. David Miln had been known to me for many years, he was Honorary Treasurer of the Church I attended, old Kings School Boy, owned a racehorse and was principal owner of Mollington Banastre which was a hotel just on the outskirts of Chester So what on earth did he need £250 for? This was not one of the best or happiest periods of my life for I was just a cheap office clerk. I worked the telephone, I did clerking, writing envelopes and any other odd pointless jobs. There were two other apprentices with me who both had received similar education to me, I believe one left shortly after me, and the other saw it through, only to be taken away by the start of the 1939 war and unhappily never to return. We were given a plot of land on the outskirts of Chester so that we could plant and observe the growing of vegetables and flowers week by week. We attended various flower and vegetable shows throughout the district and I suppose we picked up information as we went along. The office itself was situated above Burton the Tailors (Fifty Shilling Suits in those days!) which was immediately next to the well known

Eastgate Clock and the office entrance was actually on the Chester Walls. Going to and from work I walked along the walls until I came to the Northgate and then home from there which was quite an unusual way for anyone to go to and fro from their place of work. Much more interesting was the floor above the office which housed the Crosville Motor Company's Staff Club and where players of Chester Football Club spent many hours playing snooker. I visited the club twice a day as it was my duty to take the huge Milns staff teapot to be filled with hot water to make the tea and this quite naturally sometimes took longer than it should for I knew many of the players and was always thirsting for football gossip.

I think the disappointing thing was the lack of instruction and practical information and the general 'dogs body' attitude of the whole thing and it did occur to me at the time that three of us paying £250 was a lot of money which was probably spent on a scheme David Miln had conjured up where he was promoting a Danish seed called 'Parkers Huskless Oats' which I am certain never took off and was never heard of again. Another part of this training featured working with the men who mixed these huge piles of grass and clover seeds and bagged them ready for delivery. This was all done in sheds alongside Chester Northgate Station, long since replaced by a leisure complex and car parks and as an apprentice I had to suffer an initiation before I could participate and this involved being buried up to my neck in this pile of cold seeds and dig my way out and this took a long time. Another thing I remember was the daily gamble on the cigarette card number. Most of the men would buy a packet of ten cigarettes which were always sealed in cellophane. Before a new one was opened we all paid a penny and guessed the number on the picture card and the nearest one won the all the bets. This went on many times a day. At break time we went below to the railwaymen's shed and gathered round a huge blazing brazier. The other thing that used to cut me up at that place was although I was paid my twelve and sixpence (72p) per week, the envelope containing it was always thrown across the Office by the Senior Clerk and just landed on my desk. I thought this was exceedingly bad manners - in fact it disgusted me. After that, things deteriorated at speed and it was obvious that I was a very unhappy person. It was possible that at this time I was on the verge of a nervous breakdown and my parents soon became aware of this, so that at the Easter 1937 break it was decided that I should leave the employment of Milns' Seeds. It was not a happy departure, but on looking back I know that the experience gained gave me great insight into the good and bad of the world outside at an early stage in my growing up.

On leaving this employment, I now found myself in a sort of limbo. I now wanted to do what I'd formerly wanted to do or, perhaps said I wanted to do, and that was to engage in the profession of pharmacy. Having indicated my wishes to my father and mother there was now a dilemma, as I had still not qualified for a School Certificate of Education and this was essential before I could register as an apprentice with the Pharmaceutical Society. I then spent all of the next month recuperating and trying to come back to normal health and a few weeks later then enrolled in what was then Skerrys

College in Liverpool. This was an organization specializing in Cram Courses. For the first time I started paying serious attention to learning and the progress was rapid. At Kings School I was hopeless at mathematics and yet in three months at Skerrys College in passing my Certificate I obtained Distinction in Arithmetic, Algebra and Geometry. I do not quite know how to comment on this except to say that obviously teachers appeal to different people in the way they teach a subject. It was a new experience to travel to Liverpool daily and amongst these experiences I had was on leaving in the afternoon I always looked across the river Mersey to Birkenhead where this huge new Aircraft Carrier was being built in the Cammell Lairds Shipyard. When launched she was named *Ark Royal* and little did I realise what the future might be holding for that wonderful, much loved ship, leading to its untimely sinking during World War II.

About this time, one of those incidents in life that seem afterwards to be quite illogical happened. My mother had a very long-standing friend called Doris Hunt who at this time lived in Harrow. She had married a Harry Keightley and they first went to live in Castleford Yorkshire where he worked for one of the coal companies. He had then moved office to London and by this time they had brought into the world three daughters and a son. The second daughter called Norah had left school and worked at Kings Cross Station for the LNER Company, and as she was the recipient of free travel she had asked if she could come and stay with us. Thus on a hot sunny day, I was denied listening on the wireless to the TT Motorcycle races and forced to accompany my mother to meet this 'girl' at Chester General Station. This was the beginning of a friendship with my family during which she spent all Bank Holidays and some holidays living with us rather like a daughter. She was very fond of my father and he always enjoyed her company. Brother Alun and I vied as to who should go out with her and he always won because it was alleged that I had a girlfriend of my own. However, we all had many happy times during those two years before the start of the war. The friendship grew into young love and on my 21st Birthday I became engaged to Norah, this was happening all the time during the war to many people. Many letters were written and she was always at my home when I had any leave. However, one day I received a letter to the effect that she felt she could not continue this engagement as it was curtailing her life whilst I was away at sea. This was a typical "Dear John" letter of which there were many flying about in those times. So it was left like that, we corresponded intermittently and I was not to meet her until she phoned me on my 65th Birthday as we had arranged to do many years ago. I arranged to meet Norah on one of my many London visits, and learned she had married in 1946 and was very proud of her five children but had been widowed recently. As I was in London for a few days each month we agreed to meet and go out for a meal from time to time. Recently I learned that she had died in 2004.

In January of 1937, I entered my Articles of Apprenticeship with Boots the Chemists at Chester, which was at that time one of their larger stores that carried not only a Pharmacy, large toiletry counters, nurse operated counter, library and in the shop above a handbag and gifts department and employing some sixty Staff. The Manager, Mr Stewart, was my apprentice master. He was a kindly dour Scot and whilst he was strict he was very popular with the staff. In the dispensary was another pharmacist who was the one who was actually my instructor. There were two apprentices, of which I was one and the other called Arthur Barlow was a year senior to me and full of tricks. He was the bane of Mr Stewart's life for he never seemed to be available and generally produced the remark from the boss of *'where's Arthur'? In the bog again I suppose'.* Arthur was an avid reader of doubtful books and it seems his whereabouts when missing was at least known to the boss. In the cellar of the shop were the porters, Albert the eldest one always seemed to be telling me fanciful war stories and the places all these adventures took place, so that at my lunch break I was obliged to get my daily dose of his army reminiscences. The other porter, Fred, was a hard working communist and also a conscientious objector. He was respected for this and when the war came he was excused from joining the Forces. The main shop was mainly full of young female assistants who seemed to imagine that the apprentice was there for their command and usage, but in the main they were a happy and interesting bunch. Over the next two years I was fully occupied learning how to dispense various forms of medicine from bottles of cough medicine and tonics, ointments, pills, gargles and so on. I was instructed in counter skills, window dressing and the wrapping and packaging of many drugs and home remedies most of which have now disappeared or are already packed at much higher prices. I was taught the art of dispensing prescriptions and assisting in these skills, not just by standing by and watching. The drug counter staff consisted of four men and one lady called Molly, a middle aged spinster, and the men used to congregate at the far end of the counter at the dispensary end when all was quiet, and leave any serving to me.

One day a little old lady came in and as she approached the Counter a none too silent man's voice at the end of the Counter said:
You'll have to shout to her she's very deaf.
To which the little old lady replied:
It's not me that's deafit's my Twin Sister!
Which left me as a very uncomfortable and embarrassed apprentice much to the delight of my alleged colleagues.

On another occasion, Molly, the one lady assistant on the Counter, was approached by a Customer who said:
Can I have a Suspensory Bandage (jock strap) *for my Husband?*
Molly asked: *What size does he want?*
Lady replied: *I don't know.*
Molly: *Is he as big as any of the men at the end of the counter?*
Explosion at the end of the counter!!! I do not recall the outcome.

In the days before the advent of the NHS in 1948 dispensing was quite a different operation. All bottles of medicine were made up from the ingredients and ointments, pills were hand made, and the completion of the work was quite unlike that of today being more elaborate. As an example, on completion of a bottle of medicine, the appropriate cork was inserted then a printed paper disc was placed on the cork and finally a paper cap was affixed followed by wrapping in white demy (pronounced deemy) paper and sealing the ends with sealing wax. In fact, nothing left the pharmacy, no matter how small, without being wrapped in white demy paper and sealed with sealing wax. The number of items dispensed prior to the NHS was very much less than now but as indicated the attention required was more time consuming and most were what is now termed private prescriptions. The only other dispensing was for the National Health Insurance and a small contract with the Post Office Staff services. One of the not so pleasant duties was to take prescriptions which had errors in the writing to the various practitioners in Nicholas Street (Chester's Harley Street) and ask the receptionists to speak to the offending doctor to correct the error. It must be remembered that relationships between General Practitioners and lowly Chemists was not as they are today and so it was, for me, a very forbidding task.

CHAPTER TWO

The Dark Clouds are Gathering

It is upon the Navy
under the Providence of God
that this, our island Nation,
do chiefly depends

- Admiral Lord Nelson

In 1938 the clouds of War were gathering with the continuing notice now being taken of Germany and the outpouring of aggression by Chancellor Hitler, which was then followed by the production of the famous piece of paper that Prime Minister Chamberlain obtained which declared "Peace in our Time" which was later to prove to be an illusion. In view of the possibility of surprise Air Raids it now followed that there would be a need to have a night practice 'Blackout' all over the whole of Great Britain. At the time it was not taken too seriously and, to some, proved to be a great novelty to be riding bicycles along the dark streets with all the lights on cars and other vehicles reduced to a minimum of brightness with extraordinary looking masks on their headlights. The consequence of this meant that people of my age were, at last, beginning to be aware of the future danger and so most of my schoolmates were now joining the Cheshire Yeomanry whereas only two of us elected to join the Royal Naval Volunteer Reserve. Whether the two of us were not attracted by the glamorous horse riding gear and spurs may have been the reason, but that is how it appeared to me. My part time training at the Naval establishment in Connahs Quay was to be short lived, but in that time I learned the details of this ancient naval uniform which seemed to traditionally attract the public and in particular the girls. The trousers or bell

bottoms as they were known had a flap at the front instead of fly buttons, this being for quick release in the event of going overboard. The shirt was short sleeved with a square neck and royal blue border and in winter a blue sweater was added before the thick tunic with the large collar was put on over your head. The well known sailor's collar with the three stripes was added whilst on ceremonial duty, falling in for inspection and going ashore. "Going ashore" meant leaving your ship or leaving any shore establishment, because any building occupied by the Navy is called a "stone ship" and treated in exactly the same way as any Naval vessel. The cap was the well known shape (not to be worn on the back of your head however), and the ribbon which normally carried the name of your ship was exchanged for a ribbon with just HMS around the brim, this being a security measure to protect knowledge of the whereabouts of any Naval vessel in times of war. The final part of this uniform was the greatcoat and it was amusing to learn that the only way to put this on was by putting your arms in the sleeves and swinging the coat over your head, this method being adopted so that it would not crush the sailor's collar underneath. It was interesting to discover just how many people would touch a sailor's collar to wish them luck, which was a custom that seems to go back a long way into history through many generations. It was a nice gesture.

On 2nd September I was instructed to proceed to Plymouth to Devonport Barracks and commence service in the Royal Navy. The next day, 3rd September 1939, Britain declared war on Germany, the reason and history of how this evolved is well documented elsewhere. This was the beginning of the second phase of growing up for a 19-year-old Ordinary Seaman all dressed up in this strange uniform which I hardly knew how to wear and now to this was added a Kitbag and a Hammock, or more correctly a piece of canvas with some metal punched holes in it and some strands of cord. This when put together, as instructed, becomes a hammock which then travels with you wherever you are sent this being your sleeping gear, all the time you are a rating. I now began my early real training of what was to be expected of me from now on. Devonport Barracks did not appear to have altered since Nelson's days; it was a formidable stone building with all sorts of outbuildings. The eating and sleeping buildings were cold, bare and uninviting and also waiting for us were a motley collection of senior Naval Ratings who had been brought out of retirement and were delighted to have such raw material as us to work on and initiate into the mysteries of the Senior Service. Mysteries they were for these 'old' hands knew it all and exploited us to the full. This brings to mind a wonderful story of two raw recruits (like I was then) who were sitting all huddled up in the corner of their Nissan Hut with the noise of the rain pounding on the tin roof trying their first letters home when one said to the other:

"How do you spell darrall?"
"What do you mean, what are you writing to say?" said his mate.
"I'm writing to ask me Mam to see if she 'as she got any boots darrall keep the water out."
And the reply he received, *"It's not darrall, you clot, it's worrall keep the water out!"*

A Liverpool upbringing is of great help in understanding and translating this lingo!

In addition, we now became used to naval jargon, which uses word and expressions that are rarely heard outside the Service. Some of the innovations were just ignorance and were an indication of the lack of education that these old ratings had never had. An expression like "Them as is keen gets fell in previous" takes a little understanding at first, but it gets the message over which, after all, was all that was intended. I never quite understood why having been issued with new boots these old lags always persuaded us that they needed an extra thick sole, for which they were paid without much demur. Their other racket was haircutting, but I think I have dwelt long enough on these worthies, who after all were the backbone of the Navy and they must have been a great asset to the Service in the early days of the War in attempting to teach us landlubbers the rudiments of seamanship, tying knots and keeping out of trouble. After three months basic training, which apart from being a complete mind blowing experience, I was left fitter than I had ever been in my life up to this time. Now, it appeared, I was ready, or as much as

I could be ready, to join my first ship and the moment came perhaps a little sooner than I expected. When I learned I was to be drafted to HMS *Furious*, one of our older Aircraft Carriers, the timely nods of the head and the long faces left me in no doubt that this was not thought to be a best of Draft Chits, and the message I received was that this ship was best described as a Hell Ship. So with seven other brand new ratings, put in the charge of a Leading Seaman, who left us in no doubt as to who was in charge, as only Leading Seamen could do, we boarded the train for Greenock, which I discovered was about two miles down river from Glasgow. It was a slow and very long train journey, for trains were now always full of Servicemen all going God knows where, and it felt even more uncomfortable as we were going into a new and unknown experience. We were obliged to change at Crewe and whilst we were waiting for the next connection to Glasgow we were forced by the Transport Manager to go and do the washing up of dishes in the Y.M.C.A. Canteen. "We joined the Navy to see the World" or so we thought.

On arrival at Glasgow we were transported by truck to Greenock, we were then directed to what appeared to be a bombed out building because HMS *Furious* was out at sea doing Deck Landing Training, this was the exercise where new Fleet Air Arm Pilots try to take their planes off the ship and either take off or fall into the sea, or else try to get back! I was later to see this performance for myself, and even watching was a hair raising experience. This was the first experience of being on one of the big ships of the Fleet and how big it seemed to a new sailor like me, for it was like living in a small town of some eighteen hundred souls. However, the time arrived when we came aboard, not forgetting to salute the Quarterdeck as we did so. We were taken in hand by the Leading Seaman of the Mess table to which some of the party had been allocated. This was Mess 75 and being early evening, we were to be regaled with our first meal, and this turned out to be "Tiddly Oggies", which was a traditional Devon and West Country dish, as might have been expected and it was also very appropriate because we were on a Devonport based ship. The sailors short name for Devonport was 'Guz' and drew sailors from the north and west of the Country. The other two Naval Establishments were Chatham and Portsmouth and their ships companies were drawn from the east and the Midlands respectively.

I was then shown where my hammock was to be stored during daytime, then taken to the Recreation Room, which was to be my sleeping area, and shown where my hammock would be slung. Why does it always happen to me? The space I was shown was immediately above the dartboard, which meant that in normal circumstances, if I was not on Watch, I would have to wait until 22.00 hours before I could sling it and get some sleep. This was to be the first experience of sleeping in a hammock, which I was to do for nearly three years, and what a sensation it was. I don't know whether I could have stuck it out for the whole of the war. The first reaction was that it was terrible and I would never be able to carry on (I was still a boy of 20 years) but I did; and it meant sleeping on my back in this swaying thing and with most of my possessions on top of me. Later on I got a knitted blanket from home (as others did) and this kept me a lot warmer and content and more so in northern waters. So that was to be my sleeping arrangements for the next two or so years and in the morning we were all called at 06.00 hours given fifteen minutes to get yourself out of bed, washed, roll and tie up your hammock, put it in its appropriate hammock space which was located at the end of your mess table. This is where your hammock was stored and from here it would be taken in the event of damage to the ship's side and used as a plug to delay any further damage or leak. There was to be no leaving your hammock around, it just had to be in the hammock rack to be ready for immediate use if the need arose. I cannot recall the washing arrangements, but I do recall a huge space about two decks down which had a cold tap at one end and a hot one at the other. I never saw the tiled floor as there was always at least two feet of dirty water that never seemed to drain away. The drill was to take a bucket together with your dohby, choose either the hot tap or the cold, and then have a thorough wash and then wash your clothes. It sounds awful, but we managed and clothing was always spotless which it had to be to be or else there would be no going ashore! On one occasion I found a similar space with a spotless floor and incredibly clean. I thought I had found heaven until a burly "matelot" came alongside me and told me in no uncertain terms that this was the stokers' washroom and promptly left me in no doubt that I should depart at once! Another feature that I was never to experience again was that on the big ships there was always a complement of Marines including a Marine Band and they had their living quarters mid way between the Seamen/ Stokers and the Officers cabins down aft. This dates from the time when the sailors were all hijacked into the Service and the Marines being sworn in to serve the Crown were placed there to protect the officers, in the event of mutiny.

HMS *Furious* was probably one of the most profound shocks of my life because it was the first intimation of what the next few years of my life was going to be. The ship was built in 1916 as a Cruiser having a massive 18-inch gun mounted for'ard. As this did not appear to be very successful, she was rapidly converted into an Aircraft Carrier and was probably the first of many that were to follow. She did not look like the Carriers we know today for there were no funnels and her smoke discharge was by means of two gratings at either the end of the Flight Deck, which I understood had caused many problems when first converted. There was also a very small island midships on the starboard side which was the control and conning tower. Apart from these the deck was clear and in our lighter moments provided a playing field for deck hockey and if off duty at cruising stations I spent many hours in the safety nets at the edge of the flight deck watching the planes taking off and landing.

This was an enormous ship containing a ship's company of some 1800 members in a ship built for a 960 crew. I have already told you about my sleeping arrangements, but not what might be my duties when in harbour or at anchor. Within twenty-four hours of joining, I was allocated two sets of duties. The first was as part of the Second Motorboat's Crew and the second was to be allocated the duties of Bosun's Mate. The term Bosun's Mate seems to be a high-sounding title; it is the duty of the poor individual, who stands on the Quarterdeck with the Duty Officers, announcing all the Orders down the communication system. The work of the

Second Motorboat's Crew, was to be quite a shock for the raw very ordinary seaman that I appeared to be. The ship carried two motorboats, which were launched down aft and when not at sea, moored to a thing called the boom, which is a long pole swung out from the ship's quarterdeck to which are attached two ropes and two ladders called Jacob's ladders. Earlier I had mentioned my fear of heights, and this feeling in no way helped this new duty. I had not been in the boat's crew very long before I heard the order;"Away Second Motorboat's Crew". Off I went clambering along this damp and greasy Boom with very little to hold on to and then making a terrible effort of overcoming terror and climbing down the Jacob's Ladder and landing on the boat after which the Leading Seaman in charge ordered us to cast off and we then came alongside the companionway to take off some officers going ashore. I found this to be very difficult and very knee trembling and it took some three weeks before I was informed I could wear plimsols (pumps) which were the rig for this task and should not have been doing this in my big heavy boots! After that it became very much easier, but still remains one of the horrors of my life, I never did pretend that I was brave, but I also think bravery is the act of overcoming fear. Part of my duties as Bosun's Mate was "piping" all the various orders through the ship's Tannoy system and this entailed learning how to perform on the "Bosun's Pipe", a singular evil instrument which emanates high pitched sounds of various forms called a "Call" and this has to be mastered as there are about a dozen different calls all used for different occasions. The two longest of these was the pipe for "Up Spirits" and the final "call" of the day being "pipe down". Whilst I learned these different calls (eventually) the Commodore once dispatched me along with the Marine Bugler with the order to both of us "Get it right."

When at sea I had two allocated positions, the first was Action Stations when I was six decks below in an ammunition room with the hatches always locked tight for safety in action. It always left me in wonderment as to what had been taking place above me and giving little or no thought that in the event of disaster there would be no escape for me and those with me. At Cruising Stations I was on the Flight Deck as a lookout. And this was a good spot for watching all that was going on and watching the planes take off and come back in to land on the deck. *Furious* was part of a Task Force which with her consisted of the cruiser HMS *Scylla*, two American Battleships the USS *Alabama* and the USS *South Dakota* together with an outer screen of Six Destroyers. Operations were mostly in the Mediterranean and the North Atlantic details of which are in books elsewhere. There was at least one convoy taking Spitfires to Malta for their much needed air protection and this involved daily and often hourly attacks by Nazi fighter bombers. There was just no rest on these journeys.

One day whilst I was on deck when we were in the Mediterranean taking planes to Malta, we were suddenly attacked from the air. A number of bombs hit the deck and along with others, I was hit by flying splinters. I was hit in the leg and as I lay there watching my injury I was foolishly imagining that this surely must be the end of me! Happily it did not turn out too bad as I was put ashore at Gibraltar a few days later and returned to England. The injury was such that I would need eight weeks for the wound to heal so I was sent home. By pure chance this was just the time when I could take my Pharmacy Finals, and so I took this chance and happily, the result was a success and assured me that at the end of the war my studies would have been completed and I could set about making my fortune immediately on release!

During the many varied travels aboard *Furious*, on one occasion we anchored at Hvalfiord on the northern shores of Iceland and on going ashore there was nothing else to do except spend a few hours drinking in the canteen and then returning by Liberty Boat to the ship. Whilst there I was instructed to take some documents to the American army base, so getting dressed up in my best uniform I was transported ashore and then by Jeep to this army base. On reporting to the Officers' Mess I was most warmly welcomed and entertained (US bases are non-alcoholic by the way) until my return journey. This was quite an experience and the kindness shown came as a great balm to soothe the discomforts being endured on the *Furious.*

On return to HMS *Furious*, following my injury, I became one of fifteen members of the crew to be selected as C W Candidates. The origin of the letters CW is from the words Commission Warrant. In the Royal Navy, the Commissioned Officers are career full time Officers who are trained at Dartmouth College. Commissioned Warrants were usually promotions from the crew or lower deck and Royal Naval Volunteer Reserve Officers (RNVR) were usually granted

Commission warrants with the gold lace on their sleeves of a different but distinctive design. There are always the stories that go around and here I quote from the current sarcasm of that time when it defined Naval Officers as follows:
"Royal Navy Officers were gentlemen trying to be Officers. Royal Naval Reserve Officers were Officers trying to be gentlemen and Royal Naval Volunteer Officers were neither trying to be both!"

I think the latter had no cause as to the veracity of these definitions.

These fifteen would be officers then become loved by nobody and treated by their mess deck mates as ratings trying to become something quite despicable in their eyes. From the officers point of view you were somebody trying to be one of them and therefore to be viewed with great caution. On one occasion, a ship's concert was held and there was a brilliant parody, aimed at the CW Candidates in which the theme was to the effect that here were some 1800 sailors all cruising the oceans in order to train some fifteen chosen ordinary seamen who might, if they were lucky, become Officers one day and come back to haunt them!. Part of the training from then on was to intensify any duties they would allocate us aboard; also we had to attend daily lessons given by the Schoolmaster Lieutenant or "Schooly" as he was known to the crew. These lessons were held in the ship's chapel, which did not really please the padre, and he let it be known he was displeased many times and on many occasions. It was hard to describe the next three months being the butt of everybody, but the time came when we docked for refit in Liverpool and we were immediately dispatched back to barracks. Back in Devonport and once again suffering that inglorious place whilst we attended many trying interviews, which were attempting once more to find out if we were still suitable material to be granted officer status. The day then came when we were drafted along with about sixty others to report to HMS *King Alfred* in Brighton to begin our new phase as cadet ratings. There is no such thing as a cadet officer in the Royal Navy, so we then abandoned our cap tallies (ribbon with the HMS insignia) and put on a white band around our caps so that all and sundry should take note, and watch how we behaved in our training and in the public gaze in the coming months!

CHAPTER THREE

HMS King Alfred and Beyond

"Britain's greatest experiment in democracy." This is how Admiral H.R. Stark of the U.S. Navy described the work carried out at the King Alfred whose task was to train the R.N.V.R. Officers needed to fill posts in Britain's rapidly expanding war-time Navy.

The training of RNVR Officers at HMS *King Alfred* situated in Brighton was perhaps one of the important events in the wartime Royal Navy for over the hostilities period it managed to train some 22,500 Officers and in May 1945 some 88% of those commissioned were Volunteer Reserve Officers. The origin of this undertaking commenced shortly after the miracle of Dunkirk, when so many experienced amateur yachtsmen and other small ship sailors had volunteered to help in the unexpected emergency, and they had formed such a valuable part of that memorable escape of so many of our beleaguered soldiers. From this small beginning, considerable attention was given now to the need and the detail and requirements for training a new and valuable asset to the growing need for the rapid much needed expansion of officers in the Navy. At the beginning, the early commissions went to many amateur yachtsmen and this was followed by the direct entry volunteers coming out of the sixth forms and the universities. The development continued and the selection of suitable ratings was developed with great success and it resulted in the large numbers of Reserve Officers being passed into active service. It proved to be no easy task to find and select suitable candidates and then to put them through an intensive eight weeks training and finally to produce officers who would possess all the many high standards of qualities required.

This undertaking of the selecting and choosing was achieved by a structure of three training phases each in different locations in Brighton. On arrival, the 160 selected cadet ratings were billeted in the town and allocated to Mowden School which formerly was a boys preparatory school, the students having been evacuated for safety into the country. This beautiful old house and grounds was the starting place for what was to be a very intensive three months of attention and industry, and the training started at Day One! The main thrust of these first two weeks was the continuation of Admiralty Board selection interviews, a daily requirement of foot drill, and starting to learn the rudiments of Morse Signalling using Aldis Lights as they were used when ships communicate at sea. It was the early training to show ability to take charge and to show leadership qualities. In addition the training in the use of knots or sheets and bends and the teaching of seamanship was also continued without respite.

After this first two weeks training, the Division (as it was now called) moved to Lancing College situated on the outskirts of Brighton. This was a boys Boarding School of high repute, the pupils, similar to those at Mowden, had been evacuated for safety to the Midlands, and the premises had now been requisitioned as a naval "Stone Frigate".

The construction of the school must have been more in the fashion of a castle, and the accommodation was very cold and uninviting and I was more than thankful that it was summer for I had no doubt it would be very cold and inhospitable in the winter. By this time, the original intake of 160 cadets had already lost some of the candidates, for almost every day one or two aspirants would be rejected if they had appeared to have shortcomings of the necessary abilities required. The daily routine consisted of more and more marching and drill with each candidate in turn able to show his qualities of leadership. In addition, the Morse Training continued endlessly. This was also the beginning of the lessons on navigation together with many hours spent learning aircraft recognition. Every evening the candidates spent washing and cleaning their clothes and gear for a meticulous standard of turn out expected each morning. It was interesting to note how much attention was paid to the health of the candidates, the great fear being that if an epidemic took place it would slow down the continuing production of much needed officers. To illustrate this I reported a sore throat one morning, and was immediately sent to Sick Bay spending the whole day in bed until it was confirmed that I was not infectious. It was quite a pleasant day off from the daily routine!

Each day the numbers reduced as the unsuitable cadets were returned to general service, no contact being made with anyone before departure. No questions were asked and none expected. After six weeks the remainder of the Division moved to Hove Baths which had been converted for the final training. The swimming pool, after appropriate conversion, was now a Drill Hall and assembly area and the underground car park became a dormitory. The approach of Autumn helped to prove this place quite unsuitable and uncomfortable for sleep in the few hours designated for such a luxury. The training at Hove was similar and boat handling was held about a mile down the road at Portslade, this now being added to the course. The numbers still continued to diminish as each day passed and I was now instructed, along with the other remaining Cadet Ratings, to go to one of the four or five famous named tailors and having chosen the one I wished to be measured for my uniform, not that we were yet Officers but in order to effect the transition if and when the day came. The last two weeks were mostly about my own individual capabilities to drill and take charge of men and also passing the various written examinations, the chief of these being navigation, all of which must reach 50% of the marks in each of the subjects in order to be considered for the final approval.

Eventually the final day arrived and those who were still with the Division were assembled in the Drill Hall, and it was hard to imagine how they must have felt returning to General Service after the last two months of hard work and expectations. This left some sixty newly appointed Officers to congratulate each other and be congratulated by Captain Pelly the Commanding Officer of *King Alfred.* Then the immediate task was to go and collect the various items of uniform that had been prepared for you by the tailor and return and after changing into your new uniform join the instructing officers for sherry in the Ward Room. During this pleasant interlude a chance came to me to have a chat with Captain Pelly who gave me a piece of advice which went rather like this: *"Knowles, there are two types of Officers in the Royal Navy, a shit and a wet, make sure you're a shit!"* Though not quite understanding what he was getting at, I subsequently realised the truth of these words of wisdom.

A well-deserved weekend Leave followed so that along with the others I could get used to this new status and the new sparkling gold lace. I returned by train to Prestatyn to show myself off to my Parents and arriving in the middle of the night was obliged to throw pebbles up to the bedroom window in order to let me in, which was a rather inglorious arrival.

It was at this time that I first met Bertie Fry (later known as Teddy Fry) who became a constant and helpful friend from this time onwards. During many hours spent together, we talked about what we would do after the war and he learned that I was a pharmacist. Whether it was because he thought that must be a good idea I will never know, for immediately on leaving the Navy he became an apprentice with Boots the Chemists in his hometown of Pinner, and after this attended Chelsea School of Pharmacy and qualified, as I knew he would,without too much difficulty. Although we served in different flotillas, I always seemed to be renewing this friendship no matter which port was our operational base. This friendship in peacetime brought him to Ellesmere

Port to see me frequently but after his marriage (to another pharmacist) and settling down with his new business in Malvern the visits naturally became less frequent but continued through the next sixty years until his untimely death in 2006. At one time we were partners in a franchise selling pharmaceutical products to other pharmacies, and used to meet mid-way between our respective homes in various pub car parks to transfer stocks of drugs from one car to another. In this present climate of drug abuse we would probably have been arrested and charged with illegal drug smuggling! For many years we communicated and though in his later years he was an invalid and very ill I will always be pleased that we arranged to meet and have a talkative and happy lunch with each other just a few months before he died in 2006.

This now was the beginning of a considerable change in my life, for now the responsibility for practical action had to be addressed. On return from the weekend leave as a new Sub-Lieutenant I returned to King Alfred for a further two weeks' training. This was much the same as before only with more and more boat handling and we were now Officers in Training and this was quite a different status. The top twelve of the Division were now offered service in Coastal Forces and most of them, including myself accepted this appointment, whilst the remainder would return to general service on various ships. It was only later that I learned that this was an arrangement for us to effect the transition from being ratings to officer rank more quickly, for reasons that will be apparent later. This resulted in a some of us being attached to Greenwich College for the next three weeks.

This was a great honour for we now lived in absolute luxury, dined in the famous Painted Hall and dined in the presence of the King and other visiting V.I.P's on Thursday nights. The others who made up the groups at Greenwich were senior officers who were there for a rest and recreation, some RNR midshipmen, whose behaviour could best be described as "frantic", and others of unknown origin. Whilst there we were taught naval history and more navigation together with boat handling on the river Thames. The lecturer in navigation always arrived with his rubber ring,so I presumed he had an "ailment" of some sort and the homily he gave at the start each day went *"Trust in God and keep your bowels open"*, a message I was quite unable to associate with his instruction on Navigation but rightly or wrongly I just absorbed it without further contemplation. It was certainly a wonderful three weeks and on completion we returned to Brighton and were billeted in the Neville Hotel for two weeks. The two weeks were spent at the RN Torpedo Training School, which had occupied Roedean the famous ladies school just outside Brighton. When I tell anyone I attended Roedean School, they look at me strangely which I suppose is quite understandable. There was one incident arising out of our stay which always makes a good conversation piece; for on going to the lavatories, or should I say Heads, there was a notice there which said, "If in need send for a Mistress"! This obviously did not apply to us, nor was it available.

The visit to Greenwich College was designed to speed up the transition from being a rating and this was indeed true, but the real reason was that as we were going to Coastal Forces there would not be the time to acclimatize slowly, as we would probably be operational quite soon after final training, whereas those joining ships of the Fleet would have more time to improve by being alongside more senior officers. This was to be the last of the officer training and as the future now lay with Coastal Forces a further period of training in motor launches and motor torpedo boats must now begin and so the next move was to HMS *St Christopher*, another stone frigate, stationed in Fort William in the north of Scotland. The journey from London to Fort William in the Western Isles of Scotland proved to be long and tedious. The first journey from London to Glasgow was endured in the normal wartime crowded train and that part was completed without incident. From Glasgow to Fort William the journey was slow with the train stopping at each small station. Most of the journey was early in the evening and part of the night and the blackout everywhere added to the mystery of this adventure into the unknown. There were four of us in the compartment of the train and to pass the time we had been very circumspect and taken with us a bottle of gin and a tin of lamb's tongue, thus enabling us to pass the time less monotonously, and we eventually completed the journey arriving at this tiny station, which was in total darkness.

St Christopher had been the name given to a shore training base at Fort William that is situated at the north east corner of Loch Linnhae, which is some twenty miles from Oban, the ferry port for the Western Isles. Following the start of hostilities, this small town had been chosen as the most suitable base for the training of officers and ratings before becoming operational in Coastal Forces. It had a most formidable reputation and it lived up to it during my sojourn there. The Base consisted of the Highland Hotel, situated up a steep hill at the back of the town and used for some training and also administrative offices. Another hotel situated in the town was used as a Mess and in addition there was some sleeping accommodation. Further down the main street were a number of 'dormitories' which accommodated officers during the first weeks of their training, and turning out in the morning to dash up to breakfast along the main street was not a pleasant experience in the cold and driving rain which always seemed to prevail. Further discomfort was added if your arrival at the Mess was one minute after 08.00 hours the Wren Petty Officer in charge refused admission and so hunger was the result that had to be endured without complaint. I never found out who had given her such powers, but I can assure you that this formidable Scottish lady was the most unpopular Wren we had ever met, nor did I ever find such a similar being on all my various travels afterwards. Our sleeping quarters were very uncomfortable and draughty and we slept in very old cast iron 'double bunks' the top bed of which required special skills to negotiate, especially when attempting to get dressed quickly first thing in the mornings. I have attempted to dwell at length and have given this place some detail as I felt it was necessary to get the atmosphere of this outpost of the north which had now become almost fully occupied by the Royal Navy. Finally, the Wrens on the training staff based there must have been chosen from the ugliest and least interesting of Scottish girls! It was agreed by most of us, that after two weeks in St *Christopher* the sheep in the fields looked more attractive! The truth of this was never found out nor never be known.

Coastal Forces was the name that had been given to the operation of a group of small mostly wooden vessels, divided into Motor Launches, Motor Torpedo Boats and Motor Gun Boats. The original use of these boats was to protect shipping in the English Channel and the south east Coastal area from interference by the German E-Boats. At first these MTB's were the remnants of two peacetime flotillas of eight boats, one based in Malta and one in Hong Kong, the former having returned to England through the French canals at the onset of the war Their use proved so successful that they were then assigned more attacking roles on the German convoys moving along the Dutch and Belgian channels. The development of Coastal Forces was largely due to those who were the first to man these craft and their experiences added information about the further requirements for effective operation. By 1942 a number of these pioneer commanding officers who having borne the early responsibility of these operations, were now being rested and their experience was being harnessed and used by serving as Instructors at Fort William. There were many 'famous names' of those who had given courageous service, but unfortunately the chief architect Lt Commander Robert Hichens, R.N.V.R whose gallantry has been well recorded was unable to be with us there as he had met an untimely death when hit by a stray bullet when retiring from another successful raid. The skill and ability of those who served in all the branches of Coastal Forces was also used to great effect in the Mediterranean where apart from many individual roles they were often used in supporting landing operations with the Army.

The work of the Motor Launches (MLs) was more general. They were used as Minesweepers, mine layers, and as escort vessels and not the least of these was their contribution to the success of the St Nazaire raid. The Motor Torpedo Boats were just as their name describes and in the early days were accompanied by Motor Gun Boats, which were used to provide diversions during MTB attacks, but the development of heavier armament on the Torpedo Boats made the Motor Gun Boat obsolete. There were now two types of MTB's, a 72 foot version and then the advent of the Fairmile "D" MTB', later known as "Dog Boats" which carried an array of guns and four torpedoes. The merits of each of the two boats was always disputed, and one's loyalty was usually associated with the one to which you had been assigned.

The training at Fort William was usually achieved over three weeks and consisted of a great deal of night navigation, night firing of torpedoes, firing of the forrard gun combined with the knowledge of boat handling and seamanship in general. I am obliged to add here that my first effort of torpedo firing, which took place in a snowstorm, was a disaster when both torpedoes missed the target vessel! It must be pointed out that the torpedoes being used for this practice did not carry live warheads and were set to run under the target. The most diabolical of all this training was the early morning stagger up the hill to the Highland Hotel for more daily Morse signalling. This consisted of an exercise of reading of six groups of eight letters and was mostly carried out in the dark and in pouring rain and without the benefit of breakfast to help. Failure to get 100% resulted in the exercise being repeated again at lunchtime, and the only route back was by getting it right as soon as possible. The day came when I was finally declared fit to join operations and be assigned to one of the Coastal Forces base ports for early initiation into reality. At this point, it meant the parting from my friend Bert Fry (his new friends in his new flotilla called him Teddy) but he was, and always will be Bert to me. We had both enjoyed each other's company, always being in some sort of trouble, on which I must remain silent, but one of which resulted in the pair of us receiving some very harsh words of warning from the Captain of *St Christopher*, we took heed and redeemed ourselves. We were later to meet many times but we never served in the same flotilla, which was perhaps just as well.

I now travelled to Lowestoft where I became a spare officer on any boat that might have need of my inexperienced services, but principally it was to give me first hand experience of the real thing. I certainly got more than I had expected and wondered why on earth I had volunteered for this dangerous work. In a very short period of time I took part, assigned in an ML, in one of the most demanding events of that time; this was the raid on St Nazaire. Suffice it to say I have never been more terrified or more useless than on this occasion. Many books have been written with all the details and I do not propose to add any more for after all I was only a spare officer with little to do except step into the breech if some other officer was incapacitated. Lowestoft was a very short period of time in the allocation for the brief introduction and surprisingly after a short time instructions were received for me to report as navigator on MTB 725, one of the new Fairmile D (Dog Boats) which was completing construction and commissioning trials at Brixham in Devon.

My journey to Devon began in Fort William on a Saturday morning and after changing trains at Glasgow eventually reached London early Sunday morning. I then crossed London to join the train to the West Country which would be another very long journey and having left the train at Newton Abbot, I completed the journey to Brixham by some method that I cannot recollect. On arrival at my destination, I was told that MTB 725 was still at Falmouth where she was being completed.

By now it was Monday lunchtime and so feeling very fed up and weary I was pleased when the NOIC at Brixham, who was operating from a very old house, suggested that I might like to have a bath before I set off for Falmouth. I readily agreed and was directed for my bath to a ground floor bathroom with a very ancient gas fired copper boiler to provide the hot water. On turning on the machine it groaned and bubbled so much that I knew not what might happen next so I turned it off and took a cold bath instead! I should explain here that the NOIC refers to the title Naval Officer in Charge which was the occupation given to retired Naval Officers who were given these very comfortable postings to act as a Liaison Officer in various towns and ports throughout the country. Once again I resumed my journey and I went back to Newton Abbott, boarded yet another train and arrived at Falmouth late Monday afternoon having spent three days travelling from one end of the British Isles to the other. Having found my way to the small boatyard I was informed by a group of totally unhelpful dockworkers that MTB 725 was out on trials! In the meantime, I stood there and waited whilst being given contemptuous looks from these men as they gazed at my brand new shining gold lace on my sleeve. Eventually MTB 725 came into sight and I was very grateful to step aboard and meet my new superiors.

CHAPTER FOUR

64th MTB Flotilla

"So stand by your glasses, steady!
We've all got to go by and by.
Here's a toast to those gone already,
And good luck to the next man to die!"

- Coastal Forces song

This was now the time when I became an active officer after all those weeks of training and working-up, perhaps this is also the time when I should enlighten those who are interested in the construction and detail of these boats whilst apologizing to those whom it has no meaning or interest.

MTB 725 was constructed by the Boat Construction Company based in a small boatyard in Falmouth. The design of the Fairmile D Boat came from the Fairmile Marine Company who produced the boats in 'Kit Form' and the pieces delivered to various small boatyards based chiefly on the south coast. The main statistical details were as follows: The length was 110 feet and the beam was 20 feet 10 inches The draught at the bow was 4 foot 6 inches and draught down aft was 5 foot 4 inches.

Each boat required 2900 cubic feet of timber and 235 fasteners. There were 2500 feet of piping and 13,200 feet of wiring and 235 gallons of paint.

The Armament was:

Two Automatic 6 Pounder Guns
Two Twin 0.5 Turrets either side of the Bridge
Two Twin 0.303 Machine Guns
One Twin Oerlicon Gun abaft the Bridge
Four eighteen inch Torpedo Tubes

The boat was powered by four 1256 horsepower Rolls Royce Merlin Aero Engines modified and serviced by American Packard Company engineers to provide watercooling and the petrol tanks contained 5200 gallons of High Octane Petrol., giving a travelling range of 506 miles when driven at 21 knots.

The total crew was three officers and twenty-nine ratings.

At Falmouth I stepped aboard 725, at last, and this was now to be my home for some months to come. I was welcomed aboard by Lieutenant Jimmy Nisbet, the First Lieutenant, who many months later was to become my best man at my wedding which took place just after VE Day. Jimmy was a very unusual character and although we had many differences, principally of opinion, deep down there was a very loyal and lasting friendship. The last I heard from him was in 1953 from Tasmania, where he had settled down to married life and was the father of four children who had come into this world in rapid succession! His last letter was asking me how, as a pharmacist, he could prevent such further additions to his family. I never replied and that was the last I ever heard from him which was a great pity. Jimmy was the only child of a broken family with Irish connections and at an early time in his life, he was sent to Switzerland to become a boot boy and then pageboy in a hotel, and in the fullness of time rising to Hotel Manager. When anyone asked where he came from his reply was always the same, "I am a vagabond" and that was very near the truth about a very lonely man...

It was a very new crew, consisting of a regular Petty Officer called Arthur Gallon (a very appropriate name for a hard drinking Geordie), who had been in the Service a long time. At the start of the war he was a 'Three Badge Able Seaman' which translated meant he had been in the Navy at least 21 years, but being totally without ambition, therefore had not progressed to any other rank than Able Seaman in all that time. However, the value of such experienced ratings was much appreciated and at the start of the war he rapidly rose to become a Petty Officer. At the time I first became acquainted with him he was still in the traditional bell bottoms uniform, which he loved, but he knew that when he had been a Petty Officer for twelve months he would have to change uniform into a collar, tie, jacket, and trousers, known as "Fore and Aft Rig" but with still the same badges of rank. This did not altogether please him, for to him he would now appear to become something quite different. Happily, he settled down and in the end was secretly pleased with his promotion after so many years of service. We became very good friends and for the help he gave to me in my early learning days I always helped him to balance his victualling books, as he was not accustomed to adding up accounts for his purchases for stores and food, nor did he seem able to do. He was however the possessor of many unusual expressions which took time to understand. Whenever I might be stepping out of the laid down Regulations, he would quietly say *"My Granny wouldn't like that"* or perhaps when the Hands were fallen in at 0800 on the upper deck in the pouring rain, and I was perhaps a little under the weather, he would add *"Don't forget Sir it was your night out not theirs".* The remainder of the crew were "Hostilities Only" Ratings; and the Engine Room section included a Chief Petty Officer who was an Engineer in a paper making Mill in Kent and a Petty Officer who in peacetime was what was known as a Speed Cop i.e. a policeman on a motor Ccycle, both of whom had quite different occupations in their civilian lives, but readily and efficiently adapted to the needs of the time. The policeman had a wicked tongue and seemed to have learned a lot of his tricks from his "Clients"! After one hectic action when we had twisted and turned for nearly half an hour he later knocked on the Chartroom door and remarked *"I bet you don't know where we are now Sir."* Let's just call it relaxation from tension rather than indiscipline.

There was a lot of work to do when I joined the Boat and for me the first occupation was unpacking the Ward Room stores. Whilst doing this I came across three very nice glass fruit bowls! I wondered whatever could be the possible use of these on an MTB, only to be informed by my new Commanding Officer that they were 'Finger Bowls'. It is part of the Ward Room equipment supplies to all officers, one bowl for each officer on board. This hardly seemed to apply on an MTB, and it seemed a bit over the top, but the moral of that was, never to try to understand "Their Lordships of the Admiralty!" I was also introduced to the 'cellar', which was reached by lifting the hatch below our dining table in this tiny wardroom. which measured 12 feet by 14 feet! The C.O also introduced me to Italian Vermouth, which I had never heard of before, but which proved to be the larger part of his favourite drink of 'Gin and Italian'. He also advised me that in MTB's there was no such thing as a 'Bar Chit' (which was signed for when ordering drinks in the mess), and that the Navigator (that was me!) was responsible for the purchase of all booze from the supplier for which he was later reimbursed by the CO and First Lieutenant for their share.

After a few days, we proceeded to Brixham and this was the first occasion that I would be the Navigator and for the first time the use of the compass, tide tables, and all the other items and calculations was 'for real' and we arrived there without any disaster. At Brixham, we continued to blend together as a crew with several sea trips learning to work with each other. We were made very welcome ashore but made the mistake of beating the local Fire Brigade at football but we regained our popularity with a collective visit to their 'Local' on the following evening. This period allowed me to orientate myself to the task ahead and learning to work with the crew, dealing with their domestic and other problems, keeping the ship's log and generally coming to terms with being a practical Naval Officer. After a few weeks we were then ordered to proceed to Holyhead to the Coastal Forces Training Base which would now turn us into an organized crew rather than the untrained group that had been thrown together at the boatyard. Whilst on passage we were in Cardigan Bay when an incident on the bridge served to delay us. At the time I was on watch, and the Commanding Officer and one of the ratings were examining a Sten gun, which was a wartime automatic gun of very crude and dangerous construction, and whilst doing so the gun suddenly went off and a bullet sprayed round the bridge which was pretty alarming and it finally ended its journey in the thigh of our CO. We took him down below to the charthouse, radioed for instructions, but when I tried to remove his trousers, he objected in no uncertain terms! So we bound him up and after we had found a mooring we awaited the arrival of a medical crew to ferry him ashore as we had been instructed to return to Milford Haven so that he could be discharged to hospital, and that was the last I saw of him until the following October when I came across him in Lowestoft. The First Lieutenant and I were subjected to a very formal investigation, full dress with gloves and swords, and after release, being found quite blameless of this incident, two days later continued our passage to Holyhead. Jimmy Nisbet became the new CO and with great rapidity the mantle of First Lieutenant and Navigator was bestowed upon me, this proving to be quite breathtaking rapid promotion!

After three weeks of more navigation training, more sea trips, more gunnery and torpedo training, which on one occasion during a simulated nighttime attack I failed to torpedo the Holyhead-Dublin Ferry!, and many more instruction lectures, including training for the engine room crew, we really became a team and the future looked much better for us. We were then ordered to sail for Portsmouth, and with the help of my now improved navigation we eventually arrived and were then instructed to proceed to HMS *Vernon*, the Submarine Base, where we joined the 64th MTB Flotilla, and made our first contact with the officers and crews of the other boats with whom we were to spend so many hours in the future months. A flotilla consists of eight boats and they are generally worked in two units of four, which had proved more effective for operational work. Shortly after arrival, our four torpedo tubes were removed and nine racks for holding moored mines mounted on to the deck, for we had now been designated a Mine Laying Flotilla. It was here I now learned about the things that really matter, the Gin Pennant! There are customs that seem to be passed down through the ages and then become part of the scene and this is one of them. During the period of the war certain drinks were in short supply and beer was one of them. Thus the ration for one boat would be eight dozen cans per month, though fortunately not all boats were supplied at the same time. On the arrival of a supply the boat concerned would then hoist what was known as a Gin Pennant, which was identified by its green and white stripes. On sighting this the officers of the other boats of the flotilla would gather and the whole consignment would disappear in one session. The mathematics of the quantity divided by some forty-two officers is left for the reader to calculate. What does not bear thinking is that in the event of Haslar Creek drying up there would be a platform of empty cans in view or, alternatively if the war had gone on for more years would Haslar Creek have become unusable when peace returned!! Just passing thoughts.

It was now early in May 1944 and things seemed to be happening. Portsmouth Harbour was beginning to fill up with more and more ships of various shapes and sizes and there was a strange air about. It now appeared that we were to become operational at last and to confirm this nine moored mines were now being loaded on to each boat. On asking the Petty Officer in charge of the loading and fixing of the mines was there was any danger whilst they were being loaded and transported, the answer he gave was that when they are dropped into the water they would sink to the bottom and a soluble plug would then release a wire cable so that the floating mine would come to rest just below the surface of the water. On further asking as to how dangerous were the 'horns' that would cause the mines to explode I received the answer that these too were controlled by a soluble plug which dissolved half an hour after the mines were laid. This tested my faith and belief in him to the extreme limit! The first of our operations to be carried out was the laying of mines in the Baie de La Seine and off Cherbourg Harbour. The importance of this was to come later but it was a tedious job requiring accurate navigation and timing of the release of them so that they lay in a line as required by our briefing. As they were laid close inshore, there was always a need for approaching slowly and sometimes shore batteries were alerted of our presence and responded with mixed gunfire and starshell, which caused us to be well illuminated and very exposed and as the wash of departing at high speed would make our identification even easier, there was no alternative but to sweat it out and hope for the best.

CHAPTER FIVE

A Moment In Time

"Arm yourselves and be ye Men of Valour, and be ye in readiness for the conflict, for it is better for us to perish in battle, than look upon the outrage of our Nation and our Altars. As the will of God is in Heaven, even so let him do."

- Winston Churchill

Throughout the month of May and early into June 1944, the 64th Flotilla continued with a series of minelaying operations sometimes in most difficult weather conditions. It had been impressed on all the CO's of the eight boats in the Flotilla that this operation was essential and must be completed without any delay or postponement of any kind. Although this was carried out by four boats, each on alternate nights, there were times due to mechanical failure when some of the other boats were operational for three successive nights. This proved to be a very exacting time for the officers and crews, in addition to the weather conditions there was the stress of operating at minimum speed in very dangerous waters, but it was good to know that the completion of the task was later favourably commented on by the Admiral and his team.

Early in May 1944 the navigators from 64th MTB Flotilla and other navigators were called to HMS *Hornet* on a series of Friday afternoons. HMS *Hornet* was the base for motor torpedo boats at Gosport, which was the other side of the Harbour from Portsmouth. The purpose was to correct strange charts, so very different from any we had handled before. They were very full and informative charts and alongside them booklets containing names like MULBERRY, OVERLORD, PLUTO, D-DAY and other unusual names, which seemed to us quite incapable of being understood. Later however, we were to find out that these names were some of the fundamental names of operations that were to come in the immediate future. The significance of all these did not quite hit us, because we felt rather imposed upon to be spending every Friday afternoon correcting charts in addition to correcting our own. However, on the Saturday before D-Day instructions were given to collect these charts and books which contained pictures of small harbours on the French coast and all sorts of other information. So I then took my 'bundle' back to MTB 725 and just placed them on the bunk in the Wardroom and then left to go ashore, and there, totally unattended, was the whole plan of an Operation that up to then was totally top secret and almost unknown to many of us. I have often wondered what might have happened to me if by some chance they had fallen into the wrong hands! Just as well it never happened after all the secrecy, and all that followed.

The next day, Sunday, brought gales and rain and any briefing that was due to be held on that day was cancelled, but on the Monday we received a final briefing from Lieutenant Commander Peter Scott, who rather cynically, whilst wishing us well and wishing us luck, added that the weather was going to be absolutely horrible. Peter Scott had been an operational officer in Coastal Forces in the first years of the war, and although now in a shore going appointment was adequately experienced to be the one to send us on our way. For a long time, there had been talk of a "Second Front" which was the long anticipated invasion of Europe from our shores. Therefore at this time I would like to take you back for a short while to an evening over sixty years ago and try to give you a picture of something perhaps the country had waited for so long and suddenly here it was with all its apprehension and fears..

It was a very unusual evening, it was grey skies, miserable looking, stormy and Portsmouth Harbour was absolutely choc-a-block with ships and Landing Craft of all kinds moored or anchored in the Solent and beyond sight. At 21.00., 64th Flotilla including MTB 725 moved out of Haslar Creek, and out of the Harbour, the eight boats each with nine mines on embarked on what was to be the beginning of one of the greatest Armadas of all time. These nine mines, of which each weighed a ton and a half, had replaced our torpedo tubes and so these very frail boats were each carrying nearly 15 tons of mines. Passing out of the harbour on that night, to starboard was the Solent, and as I mentioned before choc-a-block with ships, as far as the eye could see, so close together that you could have walked from the deck of one on to the deck of the next one if it had been calm only they were tossing in the wild and windy evening and the weather seemed to be worsening. I have often wondered afterwards about the catering and feeding of those boats full of soldiers and how it was ever accomplished. It must have been done and just possibly perhaps maybe some of them did not want to eat either! This was a breathtaking exercise in logistics, and full marks are due to this 'silent' army whose energies and strains are not always as apparent and appreciated as they should be. I had always been told 'An Army Marches on its Stomach', so I observed silently to myself: "I wonder if they will do this time?"

Passing on, we moved out of the Solent close to the Isle of Wight leaving it to starboard, and then out through the Boom. The Boom was the anti-submarine net that prevents ships from getting into the anchorage, and is opened only when there is known "friendly" movement in and out. After passing the Isle of Wight we suddenly hit the open sea, each of these eight boats carrying nine mines setting out across the Channel en route to their allotted destination. The total journey will be about eighty miles and cruising at twenty knots should take some four hours and at the end of that time we should reach our target area. Halfway across the Channel, in atrocious seas, great waves pouring over the bridge and the rain and wind causing absolute bloody misery. the Flotilla then split into two units, my own particular four boats bound for Cherbourg and the other four bound for Le Havre and which are the two ports situated either side of the Bay de la Seine. This area will no doubt be a household name in Great Britain when dawn breaks tomorrow. About 0100 hours the four boats were closing near to Cherbourg, some two hundred yards off the breakwater, having passed under the big guns without being detected. Cherbourg Harbour was fitted with large long-range guns to keep off major ships but we were able to close in under the angle of depression of those guns, the next danger will now be when the time comes to move out to sea again when we would come, once again, in the range of those guns.

The weather conditions were by now absolutely bloody, with ever mounting waves. The four boats now reduced speed to three and half to four knots in preparation for laying the mines. The great big black things are then dropped into the sea at close agreed intervals close to the shore and whilst running quietly to enable us to remain undetected, using the silencing arrangement fitted within the exhaust pipes. The lay then commenced and all these boats laid the mines in a line, which took about ten minutes, slowly moving closer and closer to the Cherbourg Harbour wall. About halfway through the lay we were spotted and there were flashes, gun flashes, parachute flares and all of a sudden the boats were exposed to a brilliant light in the sky and all around us was just like being in daylight. The lay continued for it must continue. After ten minutes, the lay was over, and we altered course to starboard, and pulled away from Cherbourg at a speed of ten knots. The reason for this reduced speed was that the wake of the boats would be lit by the fluorescence of the sea, and therefore any increase in speed would cause us to be visually exposed, and the liability of the return of hostile gunfire from the shore would continue.

The boats then left the Cherbourg area and moved towards the Baie de la Seine which in a few hours time would be the scene of the beginning of the re-occupation of Europe by the Allied countries in the morning. Our instructions indicated that we should move into that part which had been allocated the name Omaha Beach and on reaching our designated position to await the arrival of the Landing Crafts and other support vessels. By now dawn was approaching, it was about 03.00 in the morning, and above us the drone of many aircraft could be heard. The noise becoming louder and louder as hundreds of bombers and other planes literally filled the whole sky in the early light of Tuesday 6th June 1944, now for ever allocated the never to be forgotten name of D-DAY.

As we looked across the sea to England the whole of the horizon became alive with ships, a sight that surely will never ever be witnessed again. The big naval ships arrived first and started the heavy shelling of the shore batteries and other targets, heralding the beginning of D-Day. The awesome rocket ships fired their ammunition in hundreds and thousands and were a sight to be seen and yet, how barbaric it all looked even if this was what war demanded. Our role now was to continue our patrol supporting and aiding any soldiers wounded or fatally wounded who may have been struggling in the water, and assisting the crews in the rescuing of damaged landing craft. The large casualties in the early hours proved to be those who went ashore first whose task was to dismantle and destroy the many obstructions which had been put on the beaches at low tide, most of which were armed with contact mines, which were invisible at high water By mid-afternoon it became essential that we should return to Portsmouth for more fuel and more ammunition and our arrival back to Portsmouth Harbour at 17.00 hours attracted many spectators, who apart from looking to see if we had incurred any visible damage, greeted us loudly and with great enthusiasm. After taking on more fuel, new mines were loaded and we then returned for another night of minelaying duties until our return to Portsmouth arriving back about 07.00 the next day. We refuelled, and went back over there once again for another night operation of laying mines. This is just a picture of things that went on that extraordinary night and the morning after. This brought the realization that all the action was a very human operation carried out by the boys from next door, none of whom were professionals, they were the soldiers, the sailors and the airmen, who after three months training many were all of a sudden called upon to perform. How well they did, with little or no questions asked, well perhaps just a few! This was the night to just pause and think of all the waiting there had been and the final event of this incredible Armada crossing of the English Channel in one final effort to rid the European Continent and other parts of the World from this terrible evil that had destroyed so much and caused such suffering. Think indeed what might have happened had it gone wrong. There was gallantry; there was gallantry in every one of them. They did not all get into story books but I think whilst reading this you might like to pause in thankfulness, and also perhaps in sadness and just give a little moment of time for all those who took part, on the night of the greatest armada of all time and were not found wanting.

The many days following D Day continued with the arrival of more and more ships. The continual supply of stores and troops, the erection of the Mulberry Harbour having previously sunk a line of old ships to form the complete breakwater, progress was very slow but the forces continued to be transported across by the Navy in the many forms of Landing Craft.

About this time HMS *Scylla*, the cruiser, was anchored near the Mulberry Harbour as the main Director of Operations. Our role was to continue mine laying and other offensive operations. Shortly after D-Day I sat down and made a few jottings, which I brought home with me, and form the next part of my narrative. Although I have read it many times and it has been printed many times I do ask the reader to remember this was written at a time when we had passed through four or five days of extremely dangerous experiences, and this was really the resultant reaction passing through my mind. I can make no apology for the wording; the wording of Kaleidoscope as I called it was transcribed exactly as it was written. It has been made into many copies, it has been placed in many places not least at one of the schools in Portsmouth where it is used as part of the history teaching that goes on to the boys of about fourteen or fifteen. I can take no credit at all for its peculiar qualities for it is just as I wrote it then at that time.

The following pages are therefore the unabridged, verbatim jottings of a 24-year-old Pharmaceutical Chemist who served as an Officer in Motor Torpedo Boats of the Royal Navy in World War II. It was written as the thoughts came to me on and around D-Day 1944 when the world stood still, and waited…

I shall not forget that evening. I dined with John and Ian from another MTB. There in the quiet hotel, boats were forgotten we were almost back in those carefree crazy days, or even in Brighton. All but for one thing – an air – yes an air of expectancy, as though, well as though something we had waited for was at last coming.

Little did we realise that seven days later Ian was to be so badly wounded. But there it was – that air. There were all sorts there, soldiers yes, but note Officers in battle dress with notably dusty boots – amazing. You bet it was, in that hotel anyway. It seems very distant now, but there we were the three of us, first the Hors D'Oeuvres, the meal and, oh Yes! Halfway through the meal Ian's sister rolled in. She was rather hot and dirty, dirty on account of work, for she had just driven some Officers back from London on a hot dusty evening. After that it was coffee and peace, yes – perfect peace. But there I'm rambling on and I must continue.

The actual evening before the 'party' was somehow not all that different. We felt that it was! But after all hadn't we waited four years for this? So what the hell! What were a few more hours. Well here it was and just a few hours to go, the convoys well on their way, so far on, in fact, that it was impossible to stop them.

There was just that difference. That 'Good Hunting' over the loud hailer from the Captain as we left. Good Hunting did I say – for it was one of our quickest runs. I remember feeling on the way out bitterly disappointed, for after all this good weather why should it be so foul now? Amazing. I felt more sorry for the blokes on the L.C.T's and so on, for who would feel like fighting after crossing in one of those? Not me certainly! But there it was and we went out and did the job. The Bombers and Gliders flew over us and the show was on. One man had pressed the button that had started the machinery. It took till 17.00 the next night to get back, as were delayed by towing a damaged 'short boat' back to Newhaven. What a day – miserable 7 knots hour after hour. D-Day – more like B..... day!

When we finally did get back there was still, an air of hush, the Harbour was empty, and people swarmed all over the boats and wanted information. Could we give them any? Not on your life! We knew less than they did.

Today I was thinking of Home – maybe it was the wireless. Such beautiful music in a World so troubled. Funny, but music always takes me back to the place where I learnt to love it and somehow I want to escape from that for many reasons.

Thinking of home brings back a scene that Mother would often say 'Sticks out like a sore thumb'. None other than our last August Bank Holiday, and what a Bank Holiday. Tennis and sunshine. Alun as usual in some scarecrow dress such as a singlet and trousers with an apparently massive pair of braces – but that's how it floats into your mind. That usual silly grin he had. But the flash passes and I'm back to reality, or is it reality?

Living on these fragile craft whose work is so out of proportion to their build and strength reminds me of a weak overgrown boy. Still they work so why worry. Back into the atmosphere, their own smell – the hum of generators – the clatter up top as someone stamps around. Torpedo bloke comes round singing 'we joined the navy to see the world'. Hell! Did we?

Have you ever seen a 'Boat' the morning after? It seems so unreal that a few hours before she was dodging death by inches – every man tense – flashes – shouting, and the roar of four mighty engines carrying away the boat and her crew. A rending crash followed by a deluge of water – she lurches, swerves violently and on board there is a babble of voices. Some voices will be heard no more for she is hit – this fragile thing – hit by a heavy four inch shell. Onwards she tears into the night, still swerving and drenched with spray – making smoke to cover her hasty retreat. The tension relaxes, men breathe normal, search through the acrid cordite fumes to see what can be done for those who are trapped. The roar dies down to a smooth purr and the enemy has been cheated again. On deck – well there's lot to be cleared – sadness for some, relief for those left.

Well there she is, tied up and silent, and the men asleep, ready for the next. Her next will not be soon for aft is a gaping hole a testimony to the accuracy of the enemies gun fire. Nasty mess, but its so quiet now, not a movement on board. On the jetty a few curious people pause to gaze at the hole – others nod and say 'Lucky Bastards – bound to get a few days leave for this'. Such are the men of these craft, they don't know defeat.

Press Report: 'Last night our MTB's attacked shipping off Cherbourg. All our boats returned safely and suffered superficial damage'.

Quiet and calm now, but reflect on the cold calculated tension when wood meets hurtling steel – needs reflection, for it was a mere few hours ago. Some sleep peacefully and safe tonight. More solders have crossed 'over there', the Little Ships are at rest again.

War is such a thing of moments. Today I watched soldiers waiting to enter a large Landing Craft. Thousands, yes literally thousands of lorries parked along the road side, each prepared for entering the water. Yes! Absolutely to the hilt. Lorries large and small, significant yet insignificant; piled high with war materials, axes on the running boards, spare petrol tins on the chassis, just hooked on – nothing left unprepared. On each its own particular chalk mark, official and unofficial! The unofficial ran from 'Girls Names' to 'next stop Burma'. This is optimism, not built out of foolish propaganda but from inner confidence and satisfaction of the way things will go. Eager, waiting, patient and enthusiastic men sit on running boards, on the roadside, or even amongst the piles of equipment they carry.

Every unit waiting its turn, in the hot sunshine and swirling dust to disembark, to be thrust into the cauldron over there. Snatching a last doze, buying the last piece of English cake before the adventure they had waited for so long. Not knowing when and how the next meal will come, but with one satisfying thought in their minds – the return – no, not to home but to France to wipe away forever the stain that blots this Nation, the rehabilitation of our pride and basically the ridding from this World the forces of Evil. You can see it in their faces, the intelligent and the less intelligent, they both know what they are fighting for and they are strong in that knowledge. They don't talk about it, but you feel it. Soon their turn will come and they will see to it that they are not found wanting. The day will dawn and a new World will be born for them. But it's a few hours off.

I listened to sweet music today accompanied by the lapping of water against the boat's sides. I was far away, awakened only momentarily by the impatient hooting of sirens on other boats as they passed on their way. I was back, back even to peace days again. Music is like that it is so beautiful and yet so horribly full of memories. We love them, yet we hate them. Love them, for they are pleasant and make you think of good things. Hate them because they bring you up with a jerk to reality and make the good appear so utterly impossible in such a chaotic universe. But music was the same no matter what the surroundings and thoughts. No one will ever change the beautiful things in life - they will always live no matter how many Hitlers come and go.

To conclude this Chapter I feel I must summarise the eventful days from Mid April 1944 to just after D-day on 6th June for it must be be realised that when we were converted to a Mine Laying Flotilla in April we were not aware of the significance of what was about to follow when we were to become part of Operation NEPTUNE. The 64th Flotilla under the leadership of Lt Cmdr David Wilkie DSC, RNVR being instructed to take part in a Minelaying operation covering the areas of Le Havre, Cap D'Antifer and Cherbourg.

The purpose of this was the prevention of E-Boats operating from those areas making attacks on our Destroyers, Landing Craft and Merchant Ships during the forthcoming Invasion. The laying of these moored mines involved the eight boats in the Flotilla working in units of four and each boat carrying some nine mines. In all some 334 mines were laid over a period of eleven nights, and the night of 20/21st May proved to be the most dangerous of them all when 44 mines were laid in a Force 6-7 North Westerly wind. just off thc breakwater of Cherbourg Harbour

The laying of some 562 mines in these designated areas involved some 30 operations and needed the requirement of far above average Navigation and as history proved later, this was one of the most stressful operations carried out by Boats of Coastal Forces. Apart from laying mines for some days after D-day this concluded this task and the boats of the 64th Flotilla shed their mine racks, recovered their Torpedo Tubes and reverted to their normal tasks of shipping protection and offensive patrols.

Fighter pilots of the sea

ON PATROL: Motor gunboats passing an armed trawler at high speed in 1942. Fast voyages such as this could last to up to 19 hours

Motor gunboat commanders were the Second World War's maritime equivalent of fighter pilots: dashing young men hurtling at speed in powerful craft against overwhelming odds towards near-certain death.

With a DSO and bar and a DSC and two bars, Lieutenant Commander Robert Hichens was the most highly decorated of them all, and this moving, fascinating biography of him is the work of his son Antony, who was just seven when 'Hitch' was killed by a shell in 1943.

It's fascinating because of the light it casts on those surprisingly little-known heroes of the early war years: the minesweeper and fast boat crews of Coastal Forces whose thankless but vital job was to keep Britain's coastal waters safe for Allied shipping

CHAPTER SIX

Moving On

"To the Cause that lacked Assistance
To the Wrong that needs Resistance
To the Triumphs in the Distance
To the Good that we can do"

- Anon

D-Day came and went, and a few days later our mine laying operations were now being arranged and briefed by Cruiser HMS *Scylla*, now the base ship operating from the new Mulberry Harbour. One evening we were ordered, as a single unit, to proceed to a point off Le Havre to lay a further group of moored mines, chiefly to prevent E-Boats leaving for operations from there to cause trouble with the continuing landing of stores and troops. On the way to the laying area, gunfire was experienced and the shells that were fired towards us came not from the direction of the land but from the sea which seemed a little odd. The sound of shell splinters bouncing off the mines which we were about to lay was a little disconcerting but did establish that the information given of the safety factor a few weeks ago was indeed true. Quite confused and puzzled we proceeded to the lay and completed the task without further interruption.

On completing this operation, MTB 725 was then ordered to stay in an allocated area until dawn. At that time, for safety reasons. all ships operating in the Bay area during the hours of darkness were to remain in an allocated area which they must not leave until dawn, this being in order to reduce the risk of action against friendly craft who might also be also engaged in other operations or patrols in the area. Movement outside the area allocated, would give the right to assume that you were an enemy vessel which would initiate some form of defence. Patrolling then continued slowly up and down our allocated area, which was about three miles away from Le Havre, when suddenly, the sky was again lit up by many flashes followed by a loud noise which was then followed by an exploding shell landing quite near to us. Another shell very close to us repeated this initial attack and it was assumed that we were being attacked by an enemy craft, probably an E-Boat. The agreed recognition coloured flares were fired skywards in order to establish whether it might be friend or foe making the attack, but there was no response. Being quite unable to move nearer Le Havre because of the minefields, we zigzagged about as the shelling continued for some fifteen minutes and then all of a sudden it ceased so we then stopped to consider the situation, and what action we should take, if any.

During this time, one of our ratings was ordered down aft to 'make smoke,' to conceal our position using the smoke making apparatus attached to the stern, which when turned on emitted a pall of white smoke. The smoke was actually chlorosulphonic acid, to release this into the atmosphere today would probably result in a jail sentence! However, the young seaman detailed to carry out this order was unfortunate in that in doing so he was hit by splinters from one of the explosive shells which struck him in the chest and killed him instantly. This intermittent firing continued off and on with continual attempts to identify ourselves almost until daylight. We then returned to HMS *Scylla*, with our Ensign at Half Mast, and our unfortunate young man was then transferred to the Cruiser for them to attend to the matters that had to be done. Then after our Ensign was raised to the top of the Yardarm once more, we proceeded back to Portsmouth for fuel and further orders.

I have mentioned this young seaman because early in our training days at Holyhead, he had an epileptic fit and he had begged us not to put him ashore as was required under the regulations in force demanded. He had told us that two years before when he was a boy of sixteen, he had been buried in the ruins of his parent's house during the Blitz over London. Both his Father and Mother had been killed and his one desire was more one of revenge and intense desire to repay the enemy for causing this very sad incident in his life. We relented and made no report concerning this illness to those in authority, and whether this was right or wrong will never be known, but I have always felt, deep down in my heart, that the action taken was the right one to do despite the unhappy fatal result. I have often thought about this incident, and concluded that he had escaped one death only to fail to survive until the next trial, so perhaps in the end this was "Destined to be", whatever that may mean in these circumstances.

There was an explanation of this attack upon us in that the planning of the use of the Baie de la Seine for a period on and after D-Day was such that any vessels operating in the hours of darkness would be obliged on completion to remain in a fixed position until daylight. This was done by the division of the Baie into a number of squares on the chart and in our case would have been effective but for the odd human error. In this case a Destroyer had been allocated a 'square' by HMS *Scylla* and MTB 725 had been allocated the same square by the Portsmouth Command. The eventual story of this night when revealed, showed that the destroyer ORP *Krakowiak*, a Polish destroyer, was the ship that had been firing at us all night. Due to this uncertain bad briefing between Portsmouth and HMS *Scylla*, neither of us knew about the other, hence they had no alternative but to act as they did, and MTB 725 was just unfortunate. Today that goes under the euphemism of 'friendly fire' though we did not know the use of such mealy-mouthed words at that time. A few weeks later together with my fellow Officers I was invited aboard ORP *Krakowiak*, and the apologies, that need never have been apologies after all, were given, and after appropriate hospitality we departed each back to our own duties.

About a month after D-Day, on one of our night patrols across the English Channel an event occurred that later transpired to have a totally unexpected conclusion. Two Dog Boats, encountered three E-Boats and in a very intensive battle in the dark managed to sink all three of them, with little or no damage to ourselves, except a little inevitable "friendly fire" between us! The next morning at daylight, we returned to the scene of the action to pick up survivors. Even in the midst of a war the rules of caring for survivors at sea happily continued. Returning in the glorious sunlight of a June morning we came upon rafts and other life saving devices on to which a motley collection of German sailor survivors were gathered, looking very miserable and dejected, and at the same time quite relieved to see us. Our MTB crews were not really trained for such a situation, and I was obliged to issue rifles to two of them, and with their bayonets fixed, it all looked like an episode from a comedy film, for naval ratings do not seem to look too happy brandishing rifles and bayonets! On coming alongside the rafts, a number of bedraggled sailors were hauled aboard and taken to the forrard mess deck. As we took him aboard, we discovered that their Commanding Officer had been killed in the action, so he was taken care of and stowed safely until arrival back in our home port. In addition their was another Officer who appeared to be of much higher Rank, and it transpired that he was a Captain Lieutenant Karl Muller who was one of their E-Boat Aces. Karl Muller was allowed to join us on the Bridge and meantime the crews of the E-Boats were bundled below into the crew's quarters. Our crew were far from delighted but we needed to put them somewhere, and with 'Jacks' usual way of dealing with things they managed to find some food and make them feel a little more comfortable than sitting on a raft in the middle of the Channel.

Karl Muller was on the bridge with us for the rest of the journey back to Harwich. In the course of conversation with him, we discovered he had been an Undergraduate at Cambridge University before the war and he spoke perfect English. It was a very strange sensation talking to the enemy even though it proved to be a very interesting experience. The journey to Harwich continued peacefully and after coming alongside we eventually discharged our prisoners, but only after a quite long delay, and a great amount of obstruction, which certainly was no help to a very tired crew. Karl Muller was eventually taken away by some high sounding officers and treated quite differently to the sailors.

Two weeks later, to my amazement, I was informed that he was back in Germany, having been 'swapped' for some appropriate British prisoner of similar importance. All of us on MTB 725 were incensed by this and felt both angry and perplexed. If perhaps this may be thought to be just a wartime story, I have since met Karl Muller on two occasions when he was a guest at one of our Annual MTB Officers Reunions at the Royal Thames Yacht Club in London.

Is this really what wars are about? Is it about politically ignorant politicians causing the kinder side of the world to do atrocious things that result in nations having to carry them out? Do politicians really understand what they can create, and do we all comprehend that eventually, after fighting for even ten or twenty years, we have to come back and sit round a table and talk it through? Having talked it through a peace is agreed, and then one side must always feel it has not been fairly treated. This was the case at the end of the 1914-1918 War that left, rightly or wrongly, a sore on Germany's pride, the consequences of which came to the fore in 1939. When is society going to learn that banging off guns and blowing up things does not solve peace, poverty, unrest or, as now, religious fanaticism? It's a thought isn't it, that my generation grew up to be taught at the age of 18 years to fight, hate, kill people and worse, to be trained to kill people. At the completion of all of this palaver finally to finish in the end with no feeling of having done anything wrong, except just a thought, that you might have helped to clear up a nasty mess created by politicians and, as ever, hoping it may be for the last time.

CHAPTER SEVEN

FURTHER PROGRESS

"We now move forward in a Great and Gallant Company"
- Winston Churchill

Perhaps this is an appropriate moment to write a little more of the detail and history of MTB/MGB activities. By this time, these units had become an established part of the strategy of the Admiralty regarding the English Channel and European coastline, and the Mediterranean. The original use of these boats was to protect the shipping on the south east of our coasts against the laying of mines and other aggressive activities of the E-Boats (Enemy Boats) or Schenll Boats as they were called in Germany. From this small beginning, added by the undoubted enthusiasm and skill of Lieut. Commander Hichens, himself an RNVR Officer, a total strategy became into being. In addition to protection of our shores the boats went on to the offensive off the coasts of Belgium and Holland in which, apart from denying the activities of the E-Boats they added the attacking of the enemy convoys moving along that coast. Later the Dog Boats had been added to the lightly armed Short Boats and with the addition of the installation of Radar; the operations became more and more successful. The final stage of this development was the addition of a frigate to the operations because of their more efficient Radar equipment, due chiefly to their higher masts, thus enabling them to direct the MTB's to their targets more efficiently and more successfully.

The internal design of the Dog Boat was such that the seamen were in a forrard compartment; the next compartment contained the galley, the W/T Room and the officers' quarters. A solid bulkhead was next and the first set of five petrol tanks were situated with another bulkhead between them and the engine room. The next sealed compartment contained a further five petrol tanks (making a total of over 5200 gallons, and on the other side of that was the petty officers compartment and the stokers' compartment. All this was contained in 110 feet which left very little room for the three officers and 29 crew members to live, sleep, and eat.

Conditions when at sea on operations were always uncomfortable and very wet, as each wave seemed to pass over the boat leaving a deluge of foam over the guns and very often filling the bridge. The limited electric heating was never sufficient to dry out gear and clothes, and with conditions such as this, it was a miracle that we kept fit and well, which we did. Also there was no trained cook, and the galley was always manned by a 'volunteer' seaman, which luckily always turned out better than could be expected, though not without occasional difficult problems from time to time particularly with his fellow crew members.

Early in July, the flotilla moved to Portland. It was a glorious summer period and on the occasions we were not on Patrol we would wander up to the head of Portland Bill. Here we could regale ourselves with good food at the American

Army Base and we would watch the duty MTB's crossing the English Channel, seemingly for hours, as the sun went down, and it was good to know it was not our turn to go across. This was a beautiful part of our Island on which to be based and as it was almost mid-summer, everything seemed to calm down. Below the rock of Portland Bill is the well known 'Portland Race' where the sea bubbles and froths in quite an alarming manner and to have experienced the necessity to have to pass through this troubled area of the sea was something that remains in my memory. Crossing the Channel on one of our many sorties I attempted to pass the time by asking one of the ratings on watch with me the following question:

Me: *What would you do if someone fell overboard?*

Sailor: *I would throw a Lifebelt over, tell the C.O, and alert the crew and anything else I could think of!*

This was not good enough for me so I said:

What if it was one of your officers?

Sailor (after a long pause):

Which one Sir?

End of conversation! Well I tried to help him.

This ideal situation did not last long and after a few weeks our next move was to return to Devonport and having arrived there we were briefed for the longest minelaying patrol that we had ever been called upon to execute. The journey was to take just over 23 hours to complete and this was almost the full extent of our capability. We set out just after 14.00 hours and headed out to sea in daylight. About 18.00 hours an enemy plane passed over the four boats and as it did so, released bombs. This was one of the first radio-controlled bombs we had experienced and, fortunately with many evasive manoeuvres, we were able to come through safely. This caused some concern for it was thought that the plane might have radioed our position back to their base and as it was, after all, still daylight, we therefore had reason to fear the worst. Happily it did not happen and we continued with our operation. The weather was now deteriorating and the seas becoming unsettled. We reached the point about a mile off Brest and without any disruption, the four boats 'sowed' their mines to the agreed instructions. The journey back was quite uneventful, but very tiring and we were not prepared for what took place when we returned. Because we had been at sea for almost the length of our capability, our fuel tanks were almost empty and this meant we were at great risk of an explosion. Full tanks are safe but the tanks containing only petrol vapour being far from safe. When we came alongside the fuel jetty it was just about midday on the Saturday and the dock workers were on the point of going home and refused to fill our tanks. The danger now became more than apparent and my crew stormed ashore to remonstrate with and, whilst 'I turned a blind eye', they persuaded the dock workers to refuel the boat! The day following this episode we were de-briefed by the officer in charge of operations and according to the evidence we had supplied to him, he deduced that we had laid our mines on the top of Brest Cathedral! The next day we were sent to lay a further set of mines, though in my mind and that of the officers of the other boats there was no doubt we had laid the mines in the correct place. But we were not the masters!

Whilst we were at Devonport, a number of us were invited to a midnight presentation by the famous 'Glen Miller Band' to be held in the local Cinema. On arrival, we were obliged to force our way through the crowds gathered outside. The concert was wonderful and has always remained in my memories. It was very emotional and as we left the cinema at about 03.00 hours, we realised that we had been present at something quite moving and we returned silently back to our boats. The further reminder of the stay in Devonport was quite different. When I was ashore recovering from the injury, which occurred aboard HMS *Furious* I had renewed friendship with a Jean Armstrong who also qualified as a pharmacist at the same time, and we had corresponded from time to time in the years afterward. I had written a letter to her whilst in Devonport which reflected my tiredness and gloom as to what might happen to me next. I received the letter back and Jean had written between every line of the writing commenting that all I was doing was being sorry for myself. This did not go down very well with me, and I stopped writing. The significance of the mentioning of this will be apparent later on in this chapter.

As we reached each different port, waiting for us was our team of six Wrens whose duty on our return from patrol was to clean the guns and service the Radar and other electrical equipment, which proved to be a great help and allowed the crew more time to rest after operations. Their work was excellent and was greatly appreciated and they proved invaluable as a welcome morale boost for the crew. On a quiet Sunday afternoon whilst still at Devonport, Jimmy invited two of the team of six Wrens to join us for a chat in our tiny wardroom, and perhaps be persuaded to sew on a few missing buttons on my shirts. Hope springs eternal! They had not been there long when the Fire Bells started ringing and Jimmy and I immediately dashed up on deck only to discover it was a false alarm. We stayed on deck for a while to be sure that everything was in order. Only then did we remember the Wrens we had left in the wardroom! Of course this only underlined our training for the orders were that immediately on any indication of fire everyone, including Officers, must leave the boat immediately. So the Wrens were just left where they were. Such gallant Officers!

The war on the continent was now progressing well and consequently our operations were moving further up the Belgian and Dutch coasts. Moreover, our base for operations now moved to Dover, then Felixtowe and then Lowestoft. One night, when on patrol off the Belgian coast, the boat experienced a peculiar dragging sound and it was found to our dismay that we had passed over a sunken object perhaps even the wreck of an RAF Bomber, many having been lost over that area on their way to bomb Germany. The result eventually turned out to be the damaging of all four propellers and we slowly limped back to Harwich. Immediate help was not available so we berthed the other side of the river at Felixtowe and waited, giving us a little time to rest up. After a few more days, orders were received to proceed to the floating dock at Harwich. This was something new to me for I had never carried out this kind of docking before and in very high winds, I slowly and cautiously approached the dock. When we were about half way in there was a resounding thump as the after end of the starboard side had

made contact with the side of the dock. I called down aft:
"Where the Hell are the Fenders?"
And the reply I received was, *"In the Engine Room, Sir."*

I suppose I asked for that. To say the least the answer was not likely to impress me in my moment of extreme stress and worry. The result was a week's leave for the crew, so that whilst incurring the displeasure of their Lords of the Admiralty I was at least popular with my crew. The flotilla then moved for a short while to Lowestoft, and with winter nights upon us, the patrols were now becoming longer and quite unpleasant and because of the darker nights we were obliged to be at sea much longer. One memory of Lowestoft was that when we returned in the morning, we had to pass through a swing bridge in the centre of the town to get to our moorings. It was strange to see all the people on their way to work in the town, watching us as we passed through pleased to see that we had come back safely and, out of curiosity, see if there was any visible damage. After a few weeks we moved up the coast to Yarmouth and continued the long patrols over to Holland. Early in October, we were suddenly moved across the Channel to Ostend, which had recently been liberated from the Germans by British and Canadian Troops. We reached the entrance to the harbour and after proceeding about half a mile, we were moored in basins rather like canal locks. It was then we were informed the reason for our sudden arrival and now moored in these Locks it became easy to understand the reason.

Two incidents come to mind shortly after our arrival. The first one was that the Canadian soldiers, being much better paid than ours, were having difficulty in changing their French Francs into Belgian ones, as only officers could use the banks. So for a few days some of us "volunteered" to meet a few of them outside the Bank and change the Francs for them. In their relief they were generous to us in the form of a percentage. This only lasted but a few days and I was quite relieved when it was over. But it did give us a little money to spend in the Cafe. The one most frequently used was the "Cafe Hublot" and we were made very welcome there, and Madame prospered by our continual attendance. A few days before our arrival, despite the orders about not pumping the bilges in the enclosed locks at Ostend, it appears that someone on one of the boats had tossed a cigarette end into the dock and a fire had ensued. In less than two minutes, some seventeen boats were on fire resulting, in the loss of five boats from the Canadian Flotilla, three Short boats and four Dog Boats. In addition the destruction caused by the explosions of depth charges, torpedoes, petrol and ammunition also spread into the town. This loss of boats had to be replaced immediately and 725 and others were then dispatched to Ostend. As a result of this the flotilla went on patrol for nineteen consecutive nights, which tried both men, machinery and equipment to the limit

Our arrival at Ostend, though quite unexpected by us, nevertheless proved to be a new interest. The town was interesting and had only recently been recaptured from German occupation. On going ashore for the first time I called in at a café and as in all the films, I had ever seen of the Continent, there was a man playing an accordion! The first afternoon of my being in Belgium I visited the

cinema set up for the troops, and the film was entitled "The Mikado"! This was hardly the continental touch I was expecting! A further incident whilst at Ostend occurred when one evening we were returning from a run ashore. It was very frosty and whilst crossing the narrow ledge on the lock gate, the midshipman who must remain nameless, ahead of me slipped and in doing so grabbed my arm. We both went head first into the cold and filthy water, and I was far from pleased. My uniform didn't look too good either! What made matters worse was that when this midshipman was ashore, and in his cups, which he often was, he would tell this story and finish it by saying:
"My C.O. Geoff Knowles jumped in after me and saved me from drowning!"

The final story about Ostend tells about two young girls we were talking to in the café Hublot and on being asked what they thought of the British Soldier as compared to the Nazi soldiers, the reply was *"British Tommy F--k too much!!!"*

From this time onwards, we operated either from Ostend or Yarmouth. We were involved in the landings at Walcheren, where the organization did not compare with the D-Day Landings and many mistakes occurred, though never admitted, and the liaison between the Navy, Army and Airmen left a lot to be desired and brought us very close to a disastrous operation. This was a classic example of over confidence, after the outstanding success of D-Day, and as far as we were concerned was a lack of planning for our boats accompanying the landing craft who were to embark on the promenade and were cut down by withering fire from shore guns when assurance had been given that the RAF would have eliminated them before the landings took place. I cannot lay any blame on the gallant airmen for the briefing seemed at fault, but what a waste of life of sailors and soldiers who were found in this impossible position of no return. I am sure the rest of the operation went well but I can only recall what I encountered.

One morning in November on returning to Yarmouth from Ostend I was amazed to see two Yarmouth Customs Officers climb aboard as we came alongside. They indicated that as we had been in Europe the crew had probably purchased items on which there might be Customs Duty. Not feeling inclined to accept this treatment of the crew I ventured to suggest that if they were to be offered a case of 12 bottles of Duty Free Gin, it might solve the situation. To my surprise they accepted!! There is really no need to comment any further. Perhaps this decision was just a lucky one, but it was more likely they who had been lucky. Various patrols during November, both to Holland and in the shipping lanes off the east coast of England proved to be most unpleasant. There was a great amount of fog and a similar amount of frost. When we were about three miles off Yarmouth the boat would suddenly become white with frost and the remainder of the journey would be in thick fog. The entrance to Yarmouth Harbour consisted of two breakwaters, which stretch about a quarter of a mile out to sea, and either side along the coast is just a sandy beach. Returning one morning and trying to find the entrance, on hearing waves breaking on the shore indicated that the beach was ahead. I went full astern and when safe found I was obliged to turn one way or the other to find the entrance. On turning the wrong way, the entrance could well have been passed but if we turned the other way then we would hopefully find the entrance. On this occasion, the turn to the north was felt to be the correct one and after a few moments, the entrance appeared in the gloom. I will always wonder as to why the guess was the right decision, but it will never be known, there must be a guiding hand out there.

On reaching the harbour, there was a right angle turn to starboard and then a mile long channel running parallel to the sea. Either side of the shore were a series of large sheds, which in peacetime was where the fish were landed. I had a bright idea that these sheds would make an appropriate place to give the crew some well needed exercise and so I ordered them to fall in each morning at 07.00 for PT in the sheds. Sadly, it was not successful and after a few mornings, I gave it up, as the smells coming from my crew were worse than the smell of stale fish in the sheds. I really was not sorry because it did not appear to be doing any good either to them or to my popularity!

When Christmas Day arrived we complied with the usual custom that, on that day, the Festive Dinner would be served to the crew by the officers, this was duly done, and all had a good time. This all went rather sour for in the middle of the afternoon we had an emergency call out to sea. Having pulled ourselves together, we cast off and proceeded down the long mile to the harbour entrance. The coxswain, Arthur Gallon, who had consumed a considerable amount of Christmas Spirit (and Tots), was on the wheel and his

steering was to say the least erratic. Attempts to compensate were made by using the engines and I suggested that it would be best if he handed over the wheel and went below. He was a long experienced Petty Officer and said:
"The Cox'n takes wheel when entering or leaving Harbour—Sir".

We eventually reached the sea and he duly went and 'put his head down' As the first waves washed over the deck and bridge things rapidly returned to normal and to end it all we had a very uneventful patrol. After a few more patrols, the base engineers thought that MTB 725 was overdue for a large refit after all the operations over the last seven months. Therefore, it was leave at last for us all and off we went. I returned home to find a telegram was waiting for me advising me that MTB 725 was to be paid off and that the officers and crew were to be transferred to MTB 5013 now nearing completion in the Hamble River at Southampton and that we were to remain on leave until we were recalled.

I came home to Prestatyn on New Year's Day and apart from giving pleasure to my Mum and Dad I was very exhausted and went to bed for a couple of days. Feeling much better, I decided to go over to Crosby and see Jean, the little matter of annoyance about the letter in Devonport now being completely out of my mind. During the next few weeks we went around, saw a lot of each other and I began to feel that there was, after all, a future. Quite suddenly, life took on a more normal slant and early in February 1945 asked Jean if she would marry me and we agreed that this would happen when the war was over. As I was still on leave, I was put through the early beginnings of learning more about Jean's family and to do so it was agreed that we go to her birthplace, which turned out to be Cockermouth in what was then Cumberland. This all began with alighting in the darkness of the blackout at Cockermouth Station after a very long journey on this now discontinued coastal line from Liverpool. It was only then I learned we would now have to walk to the little village of Papcastle and stay with family friends in the village Post Office. The walk from the Station took about half an hour and all the time I was at a loss to comprehend this walk in complete darkness with no idea where I was bound. All went well and I met a lovely couple who had known Jean from her birth, and they were overjoyed to have us with them. The next day we joined up with Jean's mother and the family friend Alfred Ellison, of whom more will be heard later. We both went for the day to Keswick and on our return to Cockermouth Alfred Ellison asked if Jean had taken me to see Friars Crag. The answer was 'No' and I felt that my ignorance of this famous landmark was very visible. The result of this was that it became a family joke, for I should have been shown one of the main features of Keswick. There was however, compensation for I was later given a framed print of Friars Crag, which is still in my possession and adorns the wall at the top of the stairs to this day.

After some six weeks leave, I was recalled to duty and instructed to join MTB 5013 at Southampton, as the new boat was now nearly ready for commissioning. Once again I completed a long train journey from Prestatyn to Southampton, with many changes I then had to find my way to Risdon Beasley's Yard somewhere on the Hamble river. I have no idea how I found it or by what method of transport and to this day I am still mystified by the many journeys I took during the war in finding places such as this, but it did remind me of my long journey in 1943 when I was trying to find MTB 725 at Falmouth.

CHAPTER EIGHT

Victory in Europe

"By singleness of purpose, by steadfastness of conduct,
By tenacity and endurance - such as we have so
far displayed - by these, and only by these, can
we discharge our duty to the future world
and the destiny of man."
- Winston Churchill

I stood in the winter sunshine at Risdon Beazley's Yard in Burslem after my long journey, and in the calm waters of the Hamble lay a new Dog Boat with the strange number of MTB 5013. The boat looked the same as 725, but why this odd-looking number? The Dog Boats were originally allocated numbers from 600 onwards to 799 and I was at a complete loss to understand the lack of continuity.

The boat itself was nearing completion, but still lacked some of the internal woodwork, before we could start to commission her. The crew arrived and was mostly our old team from 725 including, of course, our Coxswain Arthur Gallon and a few new faces to replace others who had been drafted elsewhere since we broke up at thc end of December. In the meantime we were occupied in making sure that we had everything on board that should be there. The builders had attended to one or two personal requirements such as one or two changes in our small wardroom which experience had shown that this work would result in more efficient working arrangements. These were not additions to the wardroom, because no personal benefit formed any part of these changes. A lot of spare time was taken up by me in rowing up and down the river Hamble, not just to make sure the dinghy was in good order, but more to prove to myself that I was physically in good order, but most of this effort was comforting imagination about myself and was far from convincing.

After completion of trials at sea and the final acceptance paperwork duly signed 5013 returned to Yarmouth by easy stages, in order to train the new crew and to prove the new boat was working satisfactorily, and eventually we joined the new 73rd Flotilla that was now operating from that base. There was the usual routine of night patrols now accompanied by winter fog and frost, and one very foggy night some miles off Yarmouth I called down to the navigator:
"How long before we reach the Cromer Buoy?"
The navigator replied, *"You should hit it in three minutes Sir."*

We did! (What a navigator) The result was an embarrassing hole in the bow which resulted in a sharp return to Yarmouth. This was immediately patched up and 5013 looked as though she now carried an early scar in battle! The end of the war in Europe now seemed to be fast approaching and there seemed very little for us to do because the approaching prospect of the end of hostilities seemed to have occupied the minds of our enemies, that it might be better to cease activities rather than continue the struggle to what now appeared to be a lost cause. This proved to be right and early in May victory in Europe seemed to be in sight.

As arrangements seemed to have been completed for the forthcoming Wedding, it became possible that on Saturday the 5th May I would be able to cable home and announce that this could take place on Monday 7th May. So Jimmy Nisbet my best man joined with me to travel to Liverpool, arriving at Crosby mid-afternoon to find a hive of activity. Rumours were now rife that the war would end and shortly after the Wedding Ceremony on the Monday, an announcement on

the radio was made indicating that the next day Tuesday the 8th May would be VE Day (Victory in Europe). This seemed to add to the joy and festivities of the day, and it was surprising how many relatives and friends had been able to come at such short notice. In addition to Squadron Leaders from the RAF, there was a Major from the United States Army, so the Wedding really became quite an appropriate International event. The best man Jimmy had by now arranged for Jean and myself to spend our honeymoon night in Oxton, just across the river on the Birkenhead side. It transpired that he was unable to find any hotel in the area and called upon an acquaintance in Oxton to provide us with accommodation for the night. I had no idea where the house was and all I knew was that this lady was a prominent citizen and Justice of the Peace in

Birkenhead. I have never been able to find out who she might be, or where she lived and to this day remain in oblivion. This must have been the mark of a very determined and industrious best man.

Jean came with me on my return to Yarmouth the next day and we passed through London on the way without ever seeing all the VE Day celebrations that were going on as we moved from station to station by the Underground. Jean was accommodated for a few days at a local hotel. Amongst all the other celebrations the crew found time to entertain her in their mess where she managed to cope with their insistence that she take a sip out of the 'Tot' of each of the members of the Ship's Company - and survived, but only after taking a very long and heavy sleep afterwards. Jean returned home after a few days and we were left with little to do apart from paint ship and polish anything we could that looked likely to need such treatment. One of the members of the crew was a tough individual who came from Stornoway in the north of Scotland and whilst helping to clean the ship he accidentally splashed caustic soda into his eyes. Despite all my endeavours, he refused to go to hospital and just washed it out and continued with what he had been doing. He certainly was a tough individual, but a great character and knowledgeable sailor, but his accent was almost impossible to understand. A few days after D-Day the coxswain together with the coxswain from another MTB had, during their celebrations ashore, thrown some bricks through a shop window. This was just high spirits of course! The result was a requirement to attend the Yarmouth Magistrate's Court and they were to be accompanied by their Commanding Officers. They both wished to take the blame and quarrelled with each other in the dock, as to which of them was the guilty party. The Magistrates after listening patiently to each of them decided wisely that in view of the occasion that neither of them need to be punished. They were still arguing as they returned to their boats!

In August, we moved once more to Portsmouth and discovered that those in charge were now able to find some occupation for us. This was to be the task of 'Showing the Flag' at various places along the south coast. This started well, but as time went on it was to prove quite tedious and exhausting and in addition by now thoughts of us all were turning to demobilization and returning to civilian life. The arrangements that had been made were that the flotilla should visit towns either as two boats or four boats according to the size of the town and whilst visiting we would receive visitors aboard in addition entertaining local dignitaries at lunchtime and in the evening receive the benefit of reciprocal entertainment ashore each evening. This naturally gave rise to the name of 'Booze Cruise' being given to this publicity exercise, which I felt was appropriate! Many places were visited by MTB 5013 either singly or with other boats and these included Jersey, Guernsey, Lulworth Cove, Poole, Brixham, Dartmouth, Newlyn, Falmouth, Penzance and the Scilly Isles. During our stay in Jersey, two young ladies came aboard and after being shown around informed us that after the liberation of the Islands they had met two soldiers who had invited them to come and stay in England so that they could show them 'Civvy Street'. We made no comment!. The visit to the Scilly Isles was memorable for we took on board a number of visitors and local people and gave them a trip round the Islands. Passing one of the smaller groups of rocks we gave an exhibition of our gunnery skills and gave a burst on our guns which seemed to please all our visitors. When we arrived back at St Mary's we learned that we had shot up a Bird Sanctuary and the local officials were far from pleased.

However we made our peace and then the four boats returned to Penzance a distance of some 80 Nautical miles, the four hour journey using 800 gallons at approximately £1 per gallon. Multiply this by four as there were four boats involved and the cost becomes quite unbelievable! I just add that in passing and it indicates just why the cost of fighting a war is quite beyond belief. We arrived at Penzance and at lunchtime entertained the Mayor and his entourage and learned from them that it was the evening of their Victory Ball to which all officers and crew were invited. Being amongst the VIP's I was allocated a very charming approximately 35 year old lady who was to be my partner for the evening. After the Ball was over we returned with our guests back to MTB 5013 for a final drink. Being a summer day had now dawned, it being about 0600 hours and I offered to see my lady to her home. We walked along the front in the glorious early morning sunshine and eventually reached her home. She invited me in and asked would I like some breakfast. She went off to her kitchen and after about ten minutes waiting she returned with a tray of bacon and eggs. To my consternation she had now changed into a white nightdress! I ate my breakfast very quickly (a newly married man like me just can't get involved in things like this) and immediately departed and walked back to 5013 where I was treated to many ribald and suggestive comments from senior members of the crew. Only later was I to learn that this lady was married to a Submarine Lieut Commander RN and he was employing a private detective to watch what she might be doing as he was seeking evidence for a divorce! I was a bit worried for a few weeks after that but I never heard any more. The trouble is that no one believes my story of my innocence. But it's a good yarn to tell from time to time!

We then returned to Dartmouth, and a few days later we learned that the War with Japan had ended, which then obviously demanded an immediate and special overnight party, which continued until early morning. This did not meet with the approval of one or two of our visiting officers, who abruptly departed. Later it transpired that they had relatives who were Japanese prisoners of War and this understandingly was all too emotional for them. The sudden end to the war with Japan came as a surprise for it was only much later that we understood the reason for the unexpected sudden end when we learned about the Atom bombs on Hiroshima and Nagasaki. When the cruise was completed, the flotilla returned to Portsmouth, and instructions were issued to the effect we would be able to send an Account (a Bill) to the offices in the Admiralty, listing the costs of the entertainment of the dignitaries at each place, the expenses, of course, being mostly 'spiritual'. After some time a reply was received, indicating that the claim had been reduced by 70% to compensate for the obvious pleasure we had enjoyed.

Now at last it looked as though we could all go home to our civilian life, but this was to prove an illusion, for on return to

Portsmouth after the six weeks cruise, a decision had been made that MTB 5013 was to be paid off and thereby cease to be a member of the flotilla. This did not really come as a big surprise because shortly after VE-Day Officers of Coastal Forces were called to a meeting at H.M.S *Hornet* and at that meeting were then informed that Coastal Forces was to be closed down and disbanded, the boats were to be paid off and then sent to small shipyards mainly for destruction. Their Lordships never really liked this 'Pirate' Unit but reluctantly accepted that they were of use for inshore operations and attacking coastal convoys, thereby relieving the larger ships for more distant and important duties. To the majority of those who served in the Royal Navy, the presence of Coastal Forces was a closed book. The boats now mostly manned by Volunteer Reserve Officers and wartime "Hostilities Only" crews and were virtually considered to be a 'Private Navy'. Once in the "Boats", you stayed in the "Boats" and always hoped you would never have to be transferred to the 'Pusser' Navy.

This now seemed to me to be an appropriate time that the efforts and trials of Coastal Forces, of all kinds, be identified, for the time had now arrived when we are all moving on, and these gallant efforts by so many young men, called from their civilian life will now be returning home, hopefully, never again to be called upon to repeat this dangerous life, but nevertheless feeling grateful for the comradeship they enjoyed. After VE Day it was revealed that from Dunkirk to Victory in Europe, the various units of Coastal Forces fought over 780 actions sinking 800 enemy vessels including 48 E-Boats. Of 81 Midget Submarines destroyed, Coastal

Forces claimed a total of 32 of them. Altogether 1169 torpedoes were fired, and the percentage of hits and probable hits was better than the Submarine Service. Coastal Forces carried out twice as many minelaying operations as were laid by other minelaying forces. Altogether some 3000 Officers and some 22000 Ratings formed this considerable striking force. However, there was bound to be a cost, for 170 little ships were sunk and some 2300 shipmates lost their lives. This worked out at a ratio of one in ten, which indicated that Coastal Forces was far from a 'cushy' job. Now when people ask me what I did during the last World War I am always shamelessly proud to say "I served in Coastal Forces". Many years later, I have been able to discover the final resting place of the two Dog Boats in which I served. MTB 725 was transferred to Pwllheli Sea Cadets in 1945 and finally sold in September 1951 and MTB 5013 became MTB 3053, then MASB 3053 and was later transferred to a Sea Cadet Unit and finally sold in 1958.

The parting was rather sad for the moment had arrived when I must say goodbye to my crew who had shared with me many very difficult months together. After leaving the boat I was summoned by the Senior Officer, and invited to become the C.O. of his boat (the Senior Officer always had a separate Commanding Officer on his boat) and whilst considering this, I knew that either I could continue this rather carefree life or I would be sent to the Far East on minesweepers. Thanking him for his offer, I replied (all too smartly) that it 'appeared to be the lesser of the two evils' Lt/Cmdr (Jake) Wright RNVR was not impressed! The decision was made and there could be no doubt as to what it was and following that I was sent home on leave and a few weeks later attended a two weeks course in minesweeping! I came back home again, and this sounded all too good to be true! A few weeks later instructions were received to purchase tropical uniforms and to proceed to join HMS *Rajah*, an Escort Aircraft Carrier anchored off Greenock; which would be sailing to Colombo in Ceylon (now Sri Lanka) and on arrival to join the shore Base HMS *Lanka* for onward posting to a Fleet Minesweeper.

On a very dull and foggy November morning, I joined HMS *Rajah*, berthed at Greenock. This ship which bore the title Escort Carrier and was one of a number of smaller Aircraft Carriers designed to escort the Atlantic Convoys. They were a creation of the war years and were of very modern construction. I soon settled down and was allocated a cabin which was shared with three other officers all bound for the Far East. The ship's fittings seemed to be very austere and of metal construction with a very small amount of wooden trimmings. Even though it was still winter, it was very hot below decks and I wondered what the ship would be like in the tropics. I was later to find out!

On reflection, I have never regretted my over smart remark to my former senior officer for I was able to travel and see more and more sights and at the same time felt I was continuing my contribution towards the return of normal times. On leaving any Command, Naval Officers are given a 'flimsy', which was a report by the senior officer on how the officer had performed. Despite my abrupt departure from Coastal Forces, I was pleased to receive a 'flimsy' that was indeed flattering - modesty deprives anyone else from ever having sight of this report.

CHAPTER NINE

Minesweeping in the Far East

"They that go down to the sea in ships
and occupy their business in great waters:
these men see the works of the Lord
and his wonders of the deep."
"Seafarers also see and feel the heights
and depths of human emotion in the hazards they face,
through separation from their homes and families,
and through great happiness in comradeship
and in homecomings."

Early the next morning the carrier started to move down river, but within the hour she was at anchor again as the fog was so dense. However after a few hours delay she moved in to the Irish Sea and going up on the flight deck, the outline of the coast of Ireland was clearly visible. Two days later, once again standing in the mist and cold, I saw the last southern tip of Ireland as we then proceeded towards the Bay of Biscay. It seemed very strange on board, the guns were unmanned and the only duty for me to have to do was a four-hour watch every other day. Even that proved non-existent for it later became apparent that none of my papers and instructions had been transferred to the ship and therefore my name never came up for any duties. This was to prove very awkward throughout the many journeys over the next twelve months, and the documents never arrived which resulted in my not being paid any monthly wages resulting in the necessity to accept an 'advance' payment of no more than £20 each month. In later months this often was the root cause of making financial matters a little difficult to handle.

Five days after leaving the homeland, we dropped anchor at Gibraltar just as evening was descending and there in the harbour we saw two large aircraft carriers fully laden with returning soldiers.

The journey in the Mediterranean went without incident, except that the days were now beginning to become very sunny and warm. Many hours were spent with other officers on the flight deck in the sunshine, watching the many dolphins who seemed to spend hours in our company. The next stop was Port Said and on arrival we were surrounded by many small boats full of noisy and strange characters that were out to sell us all their doubtful souvenirs and other wares. A few came on board and the strange 'gilly-gilly' men were now on the flight deck, they were really clever conjurers who seemed to be able to produce chickens from every fold of their clothes and in addition they had many other confusing and mysterious tricks, and it seemed impossible to understand what sort of life and existence they lived and whether they ever made any money or not! I can only conclude that they must have done otherwise they would not exist. The passage to Ceylon now reached the Suez Canal, this being a new experience for me as my other travels had not brought me to these waters before nor, indeed, through the Canal. I found this man-made canal most interesting and could only marvel as to how it had been made. Along the route we passed small outposts of our soldiers who seemed to be guarding the canal. I assumed that they returned to England in the fullness of time but it really gave the appearance of their having been left behind after the War, so I hoped that someone would come for them eventually!

On reaching the Red Sea the ship became very hot and even the effort of writing letters or notes produced perspiration from every pore,which was very exhausting, and I assumed I would get used to these conditions in the fullness of time. Eventually we anchored in the harbour at Colombo, which is on the western coast of Ceylon, and after embarking, I was transported to HMS *Lanka*, which proved to be a shore base a few miles north of Colombo. It was a very strange experience and whilst being transported by truck we carefully avoided any cattle which seemed to be able to roam on the open road, and they appeared to have the freedom to do so. It was now becoming very apparent how green and ignorant I was of this country and the tropics in general. I believed it would be warm all the time, but at bedtime I discovered how cold the night hours could be and the first night's experience ended with my getting dressed and hiding under any clothes I could find. The mosquito nets around by bed were a new experience for me and it felt as if I must have dropped in on some Somerset Maugham novel about eastern countries! I spent a few days in this base, all the time learning about my new life. I remember the hundreds of bats which slept all night upside down on the telephone wires and also about the many insects and creepy crawlies that seemed to be continually invading my privacy.

This stay ashore was short lived for instructions came to return to Colombo and join HMS *Chameleon* now anchored in the harbour. *Chameleon* was one of the Algerian Class Fleet Minesweepers and were the largest of the minesweepers in the Royal Navy and were quite unlike the small wooden minesweepers, which I had anticipated I would be joining, but they were more akin to the size of a corvette. They carried a crew of twelve officers and about ninety-five ratings. So this was my return to the real Navy and ended my days at sea in small ships. After all this time I was now back where I first began my joining the Service in 1939. On reporting to the Commanding Officer I was then duly allocated the First Lieutenant's Cabin, which was quite roomy after my former MTB's tiny cabin. My new appointment did not start off too well for on the first night I was the duty officer (as is the custom on joining a new ship) and presently there came a knock on the cabin door. On opening it I was confronted by an enormous red headed petty officer and one of his shipmates, he then muttered something that I did not catch. I replied cautiously for I had not heard what he had said, only to be told by him that he was merely requesting permission to go ashore! This was a normal practice and permission was given, but I was left feeling that the return to the Navy had hardly been impressive and the petty officer must well have wondered what the future might hold for him. Before I was settled down it was Christmas Day, and what a beautiful summer's day it was, for even at 0700 the sun was shining on a shimmering harbour full of Naval ships. I then came up on deck, and remonstrated with the cox'n about all the flags and ropes lying about on the upper deck, to which he then responded in no uncertain words:

"Wait and see—Sir."'

At exactly 08.00 the morning bugle call sounded from one of our cruisers, whose name I cannot recall except that it was a very well known one, and the Marines Band started to play the National Anthem and at that moment there was a rustle on all the ships, of which there must have been over forty, and in an instant they were covered in flags from stem to stern. This was the Naval exercise of "Dressing Overall" and it was a wonderful sight and certainly showed the Royal Navy at its most efficient and spectacular. This was yet another lesson about peacetime Royal Navy and its many drills and exercises that are used on formal occasions, and probably to give the crew something to do and something to occupy the bo'sun' lungs!

After Christmas Dinner at 13.00, we went ashore and took a Jeep to Mount Lavinia, which is on the outskirts of Colombo and just below a very large hotel, there was a glorious beach with enormous waves breaking on the shore. We just went in and enjoyed a very unusual way of spending Christmas afternoon. Whilst we were enjoying ourselves in the boiling surf one of my fellow officers called out:
"Hells Bells! I've just lost my upper dentures in the last wave."
After a few minutes the navigator yelled out:
"Here they are, they have just floated into my hand."
Could anyone ever be so lucky? After we had finished swimming we were accosted by small boys who would sell us fresh pineapples suitably peeled and prepared and all for about three pence each one. They were delicious. We visited this beach many times and on one occasion we were

intercepted by a Ceylonese gentleman who invited us to see his lace-making factory. We had no choice but to oblige and were then led to a large tin shack where some forty young ladies were busy making various forms of lace. Of course, we purchased some and after being shown how this work was done we were eventually allowed to depart and return to our ship. Many is the time I pondered if this man was selling lace or attempting to "sell" his ladies and to this day the answer has avoided me and now I will never find out, which is perhaps just as well.

Officers on board HMS Chameleon

A few weeks later we weighed anchor and proceeded to the eastern side of the island to a place called Trincomalee. This is an inland natural harbour situated on the eastern side about mid-way up the island and looks like a large lake and was bounded on all sides by small mountains densely covered with brilliant green undergrowth. The entrance from the sea was rather narrow but having passed through the size of this huge inland waterway became apparent. Nestling between all this foliage can be seen the beautiful buildings of the British residents, all of which had been given very English names (or British if you prefer). The anchorage for the big ships of the fleet was over on the far side near the Naval Headquarters. On going ashore you landed at Mustard Pot Jetty, a singularly unusual name, and from there to the right were glorious playing fields, but if wishing to go in search of nature in the raw, on turning towards the town or village would be quite revealing. The village, in common with most Ceylonese villages, contains the usual one main street with its street vendors, fortune tellers and smells. Walking on further, having successfully avoided all these perils, the beach unfolded but more accurately it would be better to describe it as an apology for one. It was littered with all kinds of garbage and invaded by fortune tellers who always insisted that you would have a lucky life and that they knew the name of the girl you would marry. It was easy to feel sorry for them in their abject poverty. Is this a reflection of the glory days of the British Raj and the aftermath that has followed I wonder? Near the beach was the Governor's home, which was now used as an Officers Club, and it was a enormous place, even sporting an open air dance floor. I did not spend much of my spare time there as I had been told the activities within left a lot to be desired and after 22.00 hours there seemed to be a conspicuous saving of electricity! Chac'un a' son métier. A hillside at the back of the town had been converted into a large All Services Hospital and I had occasion to visit there for some well required dental treatment. The hospital now almost a town on its own had certainly overtaken Trincomalee, making me wonder at the time what the fate of it would be in years to come Climbing towards the back of the hospital, there were rough dense woods, which eventually came to a beach. There was no sand here but the beach consisted of chunks of coral that gave the beach an intense whiteness. The sea was crystal clear and swimming to the bottom was a truly amazing experience. After being in the water for about fifteen minutes we were informed that it was dangerous to swim there and that it had been designated a forbidden area so we departed rapidly. A further feature in this natural harbour was the brilliant sailing facility and it was quite a sensation when out sailing to look over the side and see to the depth of many feet the absolute clear water beneath the dinghy. On a final note, I recall a visit I made to HMS *Minstrel* (another Algerine Minesweeper) for a cocktail party. After it was over *Chameleon*'s motor boat came alongside to pick me up and I threw my clothes into the boat and said I would swim back, which I did, and on arriving alongside *Chameleon* the cox'n threw my cap down to me as I would need it to salute the quarterdeck on boarding. Little did I know that he had called out most of the crew not on watch and they manned the side as I stepped over stark naked (but with my hat on) and saluted me as I came aboard. Well there was always a place for relaxation and humour but I am not too sure that at the time I felt quite as amused as they were, but any discomfort I felt was, after all, of my own making.

On the Second of February 1946 we left Trincomalee to join the rest of the flotilla now based at Singapore. Up to this time, I still had not taken part in any minesweeping despite it being two months since my first arrival in Ceylon, and I was therefore looking forward to my first taste of this new experience.

CHAPTER TEN

Singapore and Beyond

"Oh East is East and West is West and
never the twain shall meet.
Till Earth and Sky stand presently at
God's great Judgement Seat:
But there is neither East nor West,
border, nor breed, nor Birth,
When two strong men stand face to face,
though they come from the ends of the Earth."

- Rudyard Kipling

The passage from Trincomalee to Singapore initiated me in the duties of a skipper on a Navy ship as opposed to my experiences on Motor Torpedo Boats. It all seemed very similar but the watch keeping was more remote and ability to navigate whilst on the wide open sea was a new experience together with using a sextant for the first time other than my previous experience, which had only been in the classroom. This was quite a new world of action and I began to enjoy the experience. The first visible land fall was a few miles offshore of Penang which is on the eastern side of Malaya and this was followed by passing through the Malacca Straits. The name Malacca had hitherto only meant a walking cane! After an uneventful passage, we reached Singapore and once again, I experienced further sights of the mysteries of the East. Our stay was of very short duration and I was unable to see what the town looked like as we were prevented from going ashore owing to an epidemic of infantile paralysis. We therefore sailed a few hours later, proceeding to commence sweeping in Banka Straits, which is at the South end of Sumatra and close to the northern tip of Java. Towards the evening, we arrived at our destination and anchored so that the minefield was between the mainland and us. During our journey from Singapore, we crossed the Equator and as this was the first time for me I was duly initiated and accepted into the kingdom of Father Neptune which proved to be quite an experience. It is of interest to note that from that day until I left the Far East I subsequently 'crossed the line' well over 743 times, as our area to be swept was continually passing over that location each day. This must be quite a record and probably not achieved by many merchant sailors throughout their whole career...

This is probably the moment when I try to attempt briefly to recall exactly how mines are swept and neutralized.(After a two weeks course in Scotland!!) There are three species of mines, which have to be dealt with. The first is the moored mine, which is about six feet below the surface and is cut adrift by a suitably serrated cable which is towed in a special way from the stern of the ship. The second kind is the magnetic mine, which rests on the bottom of the sea and is neutralized by the passage of an electric current from a long line towed astern. The third kind is the acoustic mine, which set off by the noise of the ship passing over the mine as it lies on the seabed, but my experience relates solely to the first two types only. The wire sweep for moored mines consists of any apparatus that will keep the main sweep, or cutting wire at a fixed depth below the surface of the sea, and on the next page of this chapter, I have placed diagrams

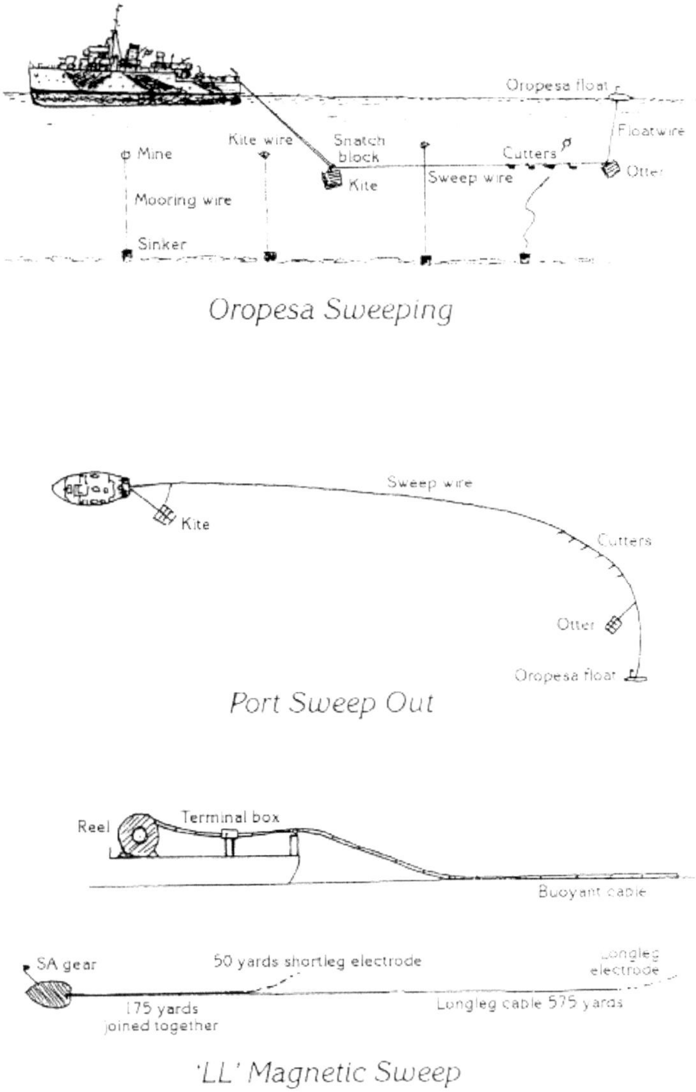

Mine sweeping diagram

to show how this is achieved. The principal parts are the kite and the otter, these are all metal and the size of a five barred gate with the slats angled either to take the wire outwards,' the otter' or angled to keep the sweep wire at the correct depth at the stern this being called the 'kite'. The far end of the otter is indicated by a float, the 'Oropesa' which floats above the otter on the sea surface, giving a sign that all is in order.

Having attempted to give a brief explanation I now return to the narrative. The first night at anchor was quite wild with a very choppy sea running. We weighed anchor at 06.00, whilst it was still dark and by the time we were on the move the sun had risen as it was was already a bright and warm sunny day As we moved off for the commencement of the sweep, all watertight doors had been closed, which was a precaution in the event of any dangerous explosions, taking place too close to the ship. At the end of the day when we were once more anchored it needs no imagination to understand the considerable heat below decks, and this tended to ruin the second gin and tonic as the ice melted so quickly even whilst drinking the first!.. As I have mentioned we were now at work and sweeping commenced as soon as we were at the edge of the minefield and *Chameleon* was the first to 'draw blood,' our first mine was disposed of by the rifle fire of the ship immediately astern of us.. Later on, towards evening, we exploded a mine near to and it quite shook us, and I also remember that on the next day we had the misfortune to get one stuck in our sweep, which eventually resulted in us having to cut the wire adrift and also explode the mine. The week continued with this daily task and at the weekend the flotilla anchored near a place called Muntock. We were unable to go ashore due to the restless conditions existing in the new country of Indonesia following the joining of Java and Sumatra; a political change which seemed to be having a somewhat stormy beginning.

Near miss! A floating mine

The sweeping continued for many weeks and we anchored off many uninhabited small islands at the weekend, and by 21st February had disposed of some seventy mines before returning to Singapore. This time I was able to go ashore, partly on business and in the evenings partly for pleasure. I well remember mostly the cleanliness of the port, though I do recall that on landing at the jetty, the road to town passed over a bridge and this crossed over an evil smelling creek containing many, many sampans. This was the home of many of the Chinese population and cleanliness seemed

to be totally absent, but I did get the feeling this was only an illusion chiefly caused by the apparent congestion and the smell. I hardly need add it was christened "Shit Creek". After passing over this bridge the town and port developed into an almost European atmosphere and we experienced the famous Raffles Hotel and near to the wonderful church , or was it a Cathedral, further on we spent many hours at the Tanglin Club now I believe called the Tanglin Hotel. After a few days in port, the flotilla received a visit (or was it an inspection?) from the Flag Officer Malaya and Near East, and on introducing him to my officers the Admiral asked each one of them in turn what ships they had been on before arrival here. Each one of them replied that they had come from Coastal Forces. This he did not seem to understand or please him and he said to me on leaving:
"Haven't you got anyone here in the Royal Navy!"
All I could do was just look at him as if I was unable to understand what he was saying. But I did! And it seemed as though our reputation had followed us to the East.

A few weeks later, the flotilla returned to Banka Straits but *Chameleon* remained behind for docking and repainting; and the much appreciated cleaning of our bilges by Japanese prisoners who had not yet been returned home. Their work was superb and they appeared quite happy to be doing something useful. During this stay in Singapore, I met up with Jimmy Nisbet my best man, who was also in command of a sweeper. He had obtained an invitation to attend a reception at the French Embassy. On arrival, we were part of a very large crowd chiefly of French officers and many charming ladies. We drank our gins with two of them and then all the guests seemed to be moving upstairs. The two ladies we were with invited us to go up with them. Jimmy gave me one look and that was enough!! We collected our caps, returned to *Chameleon* and spent the rest of the evening drinking, and safe. I still believe our suspicions were correct and never doubted our experienced avoidance of dangers unknown!

Chameleon later rejoined the flotilla off Sumatra and being in need of more fuel we sailed up the river to Palembang, which was a journey of some forty miles of narrow passage through overhanging jungle. This place,when we reached it was once the main area of operation of the Dutch Eastern Oil Industry and whilst refueling we were able to go ashore and use the huge open air swimming pool,which was still working. For our safety we were guarded from the warmongering Indonesian rebels by Japanese prisoners of war who protected us from attack by them as these rebels were quite happy to take pot shots at anyone. There were four Japanese prisoners each side of the swimming pool and members of the crew enjoyed swimming up and down because each time they passed one of these prisoners they bowed their heads in salute! This couldn't go on for ever so I stopped it before there was trouble. Nevertheless it was an interesting diversion for the crew and possibly very good for morale. Whilst still at anchor in Palembang we were attacked one night by Indonesian rebels who having cut us adrift in a fast moving river left us stranded and drifting down river and then disappeared. We were able to sort things out and secured once more. A few days later a Lieutenant and four British soldiers arrived bringing with them three prisoners, these being the ones who had attacked us. The Lieutenant told me that he thought it appropriate that we shoot them! The officer announced his men usually dealt with these matters. Now "Jolly Jack" is not quite used to this sort of thing and I could see the look on the coxn's face. With a little bargaining I persuaded the army fellows that we would gracefully leave it to them as they were their prisoners! Happily that was the end of that little dilemma, but I learned from this army officer that at the end of the war they were serving in this vicinity and seemed to have been left behind and forgotten for the time being. I was very sorry for them and later I was relieved to hear that they had been "rescued".

During our latest visit to Banka Straits I recalled that we had some trouble with the propellers and our engineer officer (ex Coastal Forces) put on diving gear and went down to have a look. Within a few minutes, we felt that something was wrong and we brought him up only to find out he had what appeared to have been a heart attack and had died. This was indeed a shock and our doctor was then obliged to carry out a "post mortem" examination. Because he was aware that I was a pharmacist, he asked me to assist and so, with the aid of a bottle of Scotch from which we took many gulps, and in a temperature of over 100 degrees Fahrenheit, he carried out his examination only to find that the poor fellow had a very enlarged heart. The result of this was that, as was the custom, we were obliged to bury him at sea and it was appropriate that as the captain I would be obliged to conduct the appropriate service before disposal of his body over the ship's side in the traditional way. I found this very emotional. It is a strange custom and left me with disturbed thoughts. The total finality seemed quite wrong for me to be involved with, and in the end I suppose I must put it down to one of those life experiences, which rarely do not occur to many and in the end maybe extended some of the meaning of the unknown and varied pattern of life. with it's many unsolved mysteries.

By now the Royal Navy was well into it's return to peacetime routine and I was by now the only RNVR skipper left in the flotilla. This meant that as Junior CO, *Chameleon* would become "Tail Arse Charlie" and would now be the ship that tidied up after the day's sweeping. This meant the collection of all the "Dan Buoys" which were used as markers whilst sweeping. This added an extra half hour after all the rest had anchored for the night. The outcome of this was that we had two "wags" amongst the seamen who when we came to anchor stood on the foredeck and shouted up to the bridge:
"Why to we have to have the only RNVR F—king Skipper in the Flotilla!"
This of course was all taken in good spirit, and I felt it was a compliment to me that they felt we had such good relationship on board and a continuing sense of humour which appeared to have disappeared on some of the other ships. A further manifestation of the change was illustrated by the new senior officer of the flotilla sending an order to all the ships to the effect that
"All Midshipmen in the Flotilla will make Morse to each other on the ship's Funnels, whilst proceeding to the anchorage!" Peacetime had arrived with a vengeance.

After further weeks of sweeping, the time came in August when the signal came through ordering my return home for discharge from the Navy. I was accordingly allocated a berth on an army troopship along with some ten other naval officers. We were the odd boys, and each of us managed to smuggle a case of Gin for our use on the way back! As a group of Naval Officers we were rather incensed to have to report for boat drill and having chastised someone we thought was a sergeant found to our chagrin he was a major! The outcome was an appearance before the troop commander who told us in no uncertain terms that if we continued to misbehave he would put us ashore at Colombo and we could find our own way home. Many years afterwards, I discovered that *Chameleon* commenced to return to England to pay off some two weeks later and if only my discharge had come then, I could have made the three months journey back under my own steam and with my own crew. Alas, it was not to be.

So the day came when we left Singapore in boiling sunshine and sent off in style by the band of the Gurkha regiment. A fine stylish send off it certainly was. After three weeks on this horrible troopship,during which we played bridge, won lots of imaginary money, and drank the gin, cautiously sharing some of it with the nursing sisters on board, this causing even more friction with the returning Army Officers. We arrived in Southampton docks to a deluge of rain and the welcome was provided by the band of the Army Catering Corps, playing "We'll Gather Lilacs in the Spring Again" - what a welcome return home and what an inappropriate end to my war service in the Royal Navy. The troop commander then ordered our baggage to be put ashore and we were given travel warrants all within two hours of docking. The soldiers were all to remain on board until the next day. Did I get the feeling we were not wanted? This suited us very well, so off we went to London, one more drink together, and then we parted and went on our respective journeys. I arrived in Liverpool Lime Street Station at five o'clock in the morning; I had insufficient money for a taxi so I waited for the first train to Meols. On arrival at the Meols Station, some kind person, totally unknown to me, helped me with my luggage to Roman Road. Home at last. "Home is the Sailor Home from the Sea" but No. On arrival Jean's Mother informed me that Jean had taken an appointment to a pharmacy in Loughborough (in the Midlands). So I packed up my luggage once again took to the train again and arrived in Loughborough Station at about 4 pm and there awaited the arrival of Jean.

CHAPTER ELEVEN

Back Home

"The buds of worry and care fly above your head, this you cannot change. But that they build nests in your hair, that you can prevent."

- Chinese Proverb

I stood on the platform on Loughborough Station in the silence that remained after the train had long disappeared on it's journey to London. I had now been in England less than twenty-four hours and in that time had travelled through the night to Liverpool only to find out that my destination to meet up with Jean should have been Loughborough, in Leicestershire Whilst standing there waiting for Jean, it occurred to me that back here at home peacetime routine had returned many months ago. The Victory Parade had been held, and a new Labour Government was now in charge of affairs. All this had by-passed me whilst I was away in the Far East sweeping mines, and so in my mind this was, for me, just the beginning of my return to normality, even if it was a little late. It was all very strange and apprehension grew as I waited for Jean to collect me after she had finished her work, though I found it hard to understand this feeling.

Perhaps this is probably the appropriate time when I should attempt to explain why Jean had taken an appointment with a pharmacy organization called "Jacksons Chemists (Coventry) Ltd." The association with the name Coventry tended to confuse the issue, but the new owner of this chemists shop in Loughborough was a Mr Jackson who was a high flying scrap dealer in Coventry. After the blitz of Coventry he had been appointed by the Home Office to arrange the clearing of all the debris following the bombing. This, he apparently carried out very efficiently, and he profited greatly and as a result he was also awarded an 'OBE' which I am sure could well have been richly deserved. The connection with Jean arose out of conversations between Mr Jackson and Jean's Uncle Jack who at that time was the chief civil servant in the Home Office during the clearing up of Coventry. Arising out of talks with each other, and Jean's uncle being aware of and interested in our future, he proposed an arrangement whereby I could accept an appointment to manage this Pharmacy in Loughborough which Mr Jackson had only recently purchased, and for Jean to take over until I returned. I was later informed that a salary of £500 per year would be paid, and this was very generous in 1946, and he had also agreed to pay us both whilst I was adjusting to my return to my profession. This was a very kind and thoughtful gesture, although I always felt that I should have been more involved in the consultation before any final decision to accept had been made. I was also not quite sure that I wanted to live and work in the Midlands rather than in the north west which I knew it so well, and going to live there seemed to be entering into unknown territory too soon after six years of unsettled life.

Eventually the time came when Jean arrived at the station, and then, gathering all my luggage we went by taxi to a large house at 108 Knighthorpe Road which was on the outskirts of the town, where Jean had found a flat which proved to be quite adequate until we could find a house of our own. After a few days I went to the pharmacy to start my rehabilitation with my profession, whilst still in uniform and not yet released by the Admiralty. As luck would have it, on the third day I was working there we had a visit from one of the Pharmaceutical Society's Inspectors and he asked me why my certificate was not on display, this being a legal requirement, and I informed him that the glass to the frame had been broken whilst in transit. He was very rude and told me that that was the 'usual' excuse! After some discussion, in which amongst other things I informed him that I had only been in England less than a week, he became satisfied and went on his way. but I was left somewhat displeased at his behaviour as I had been away for six years and felt I could have expected a little consideration and tolerance after all my efforts and experiences during those years. This was certainly not a good beginning,

After a few weeks, I was summoned to the Admiralty in London and duly received my discharge, though not my RNVR Commission, as I was to be retained on the Reserve and liable to be recalled in the event of an emergency. I was then instructed to report to a depot somewhere in Leeds to collect my 'demob' suit and other items which I did, and collected a herring bone tweed suit, a pair of shoes, socks, vests and a trilby hat! Now I was fitted up to be a civilian once again and and, as such, I made my way back to Loughborough. The business that I was now to manage was a private pharmacy trading under the name of 'C.M. Joyce' and this was the maiden name of the former owner. She was very much alive and very alert and she visited the pharmacy frequently. She had married a dentist named Lord Clifford Holt who operated his practice in the rooms above the pharmacy. He had been christened this unusual and strange name 'Lord' which caused great confusion at times and also some merriment at others! He had been registered as a dentist after the Great War when many like him were excused their final examinations, but this was in no way any reflection on his professional skills, though he never seemed to somehow reflect the normal image of his calling. It now became necessary for me to attend a refresher course and I made arrangements for the next available one which was to be held at Bradford University. The course was of four weeks duration and I came home each weekend. I am not sure that it was of much help and all of us attending felt very cooped up and not really quite sure whether this revision was necessary or even if it was going to be of use to us The last weekend of the course eventually came to an end, and then I found I was unable to catch the train back to Loughborough as the Bradford Railway Station was flooded, due to a heavy cloudburst during the day which now meant that I had to take a bus to Huddersfield and then resume the remainder of the journey by train. Subsequently I found out that the station had never been flooded before and has not ever been since! The refresher course had proved to be very long winded and heavy going, but it was enlivened by the comradeship of other returning pharmacists and we made the best of this compulsory refresher on our return to normality.

A few weeks later I received a very pleasant visit from my old friend Bert Fry and he came to see us and stayed for a few days many times over the next few years. It was good to see the continuation of this friendship but the visits became less frequent after he married and settled down in Malvern Another happy occasion was the weekend when my father and mother came and stayed for a few days in the local Hotel. I had seen very little of them since my return and so a happy weekend was spent in their company but sadly, this was the last time I was to meet my father though at the time I did not realize how unwell he was, nor did he attempt to show any signs of the distress that was to come so soon afterwards. A week before that visit Jean and I had at last discovered a house we would like to buy. The price of the semi detached house was £1800 (which was a lot of money in 1946) and I signed a cheque for the deposit in the sum of £200. As any money I might possess was still owing to me by the Navy and was still not to hand I phoned my father and asked him to transfer this amount into to my account to cover the deposit. He immediately dealt with this, but I have often wondered how I expected him to have that sum readily available for immediate release to me. The mortgage fee to cover repayments for the purchase of the house amounted to £9-12s-8d per month for 25 years. As a contrast with today, in the year 2008 an equivalent house would cost about £250,000 and a similar deposit required would be £25,000! When all details were completed we moved in to our first home at 8 Outwoods Drive which was on the outskirts of the town but easily accessible by a very frequent bus service, in very old pre-war buses. As we settled down into our first home I suppose this marked the real commencement of our married life.

The winter of 1946 was one of the worst in living memory and the snow and ice continued into April of the next year. During that time, I undertook considerable decoration of our new house and when the thaw eventually came in April I discovered that snow that had entered under the roof had started to thaw, and the whole of our bedroom ceiling was ruined and the work had to be done all over again. Early in January, I was devastated to learn of the death of my father and so I journeyed to Prestatyn for the funeral. This had a profound effect on me for this was a loss that I felt very deeply and only then did I realise that I had seen so very little of him during the war years and I felt as though I had been cheated by his being taken away so soon after his retirement. My father was a remarkable man and his whole life seemed to have been spent looking after his widowed mother and his brothers and then his own wife and my brother and I. He moved to Chester so that both his sons could get the best education and it seemed a cruel blow when both of us Alun at 21 and me at just 19 years were taken away to the Second World War so soon after the end of the Great War in 1918. I know he felt this deeply and must have lived his latter years continually hoping for our safe return. This did eventually happen but all too late and I am sure that the total strain of this and the pressure of his employment was the cause of his early death only 63 years into his life. He never knew the pleasure of his retirement years which he had always dreamed about over so many many years, in fact I cannot ever remember any time when he did not talk about it. At that time the dream of many from the Lancashire manufacturing towns was to retire and live by the sea along the Welsh coast, but to so many it proved to be short lived, chiefly because the change of environment was so different and it was just not one long holiday as they had always dreamed it would be...

The continuing discomfort of rationing of food was still in force, fuel was scarce and there were electrical power cuts during the day. I was still very much troubled with the loss of weight brought on by the tropics and to add to this I developed enormous chilblains on all my fingers chiefly brought on by this dreadful first winter and the continuing freezing weather. This made the running of the pharmacy very difficult, not helped by wearing lots of clothes and even overcoats and with the continual power cuts throughout the day. I was continuing to learn about my new life of managing a pharmacy never having done this before, but the skills acquired during my service in the Royal Navy years were a great help on personnel matters. The other skills grew by experience as each week passed and added this was my intensive studying at home in the evenings. It came as no surprise when the local Sea Cadet Committee with a view to making use of my experience and services approached me. This I readily agreed to do and found myself amongst a dedicated team of some quite elderly Sea Cadet Officers who had been running a unit of some 150 Cadets including a band of some 30 Cadets, throughout the war years. This was quite a new experience and also included leading the parade of band and cadets on their bi-monthly Sunday church parade through the town. To be in a sea cadet unit in the middle of the country was quite an experience, but we managed to do the boat training on a small stream that ran alongside the headquarters. It was not very effective but it at least taught them how to row and the knowledge of the various orders and instructions. At that time units of Sea cadets were very prolific in the Midlands and every year a band festival was held. Later in 1948 this was held in Loughborough and it was a fine sight to see some seventeen bands marching to the local football ground where the competition was held, and I am well able to remember this particular Saturday because it was the day that John was born, and, of course I missed the finale of the band competition, but the more important and wonderful arrival of my son obviously took precedence.

The next months passed very quickly, we made many friends and visited various places in the countryside of Leicestershire, and in the autumn we were happy to learn that Jean was pregnant and we now looked forward to the arrival of our firstborn some time in June of next year. This 'next year' came very quickly and early in June Jean's Mother arrived with Elizabeth her companion to stay over the next few weeks. In the early morning of 12th June, Jean gave birth to a son to whom we gave the names of John Geoffrey, thus bringing satisfaction and contentment to both families! All this took place in a very nice private nursing home ably managed by an ex-RAF nursing sister and later on in August, John was christened at St John's Church in Meols followed by a great family get together. My usual silent brother, brought along his fiancee whom we had not met before and she was naturally was obliged to go through the ceremony of introduction to all the relatives. She proved to be very talkative and forthcoming with a very prominent Welsh accent which was such a contrast to Alun with his inevitable silence. The year 1948 also saw the start of the National Health Service on 1st July, making John to be one of the last to be brought into the world before this a momentous change. Overnight the delivery of medical services to the public without cost seemed quite remarkable and the arrival of 'Free Medicines for all' caused absolute chaos over the next few months. The all-embracing service came about following the delivery of the Beveridge Report in 1943, which was adopted by the newly elected Labour Government and brought into being by Aneurin Bevan the new Health Minister.

The first notable change in the pharmacies was the enormous demand for dressings, medicine and other related requirements. Whereas the pharmacy in Loughborough was dispensing about 30 prescriptions a day, this suddenly became 30 prescriptions an hour! Cotton wool went out in large quantities and spirits (scotch whisky and gin) were also allowable. This had to be corrected and rapid changes came about once it was realised that the interpretation of the Health Service Act would require considerable modification.. The advent of "cuts" was inevitable and I recall being at a chemist's conference in London a few years later, when one of the Delegates called to the chairman:
"What did the dentists do when the cuts in payment were imposed on them?"
The Chairman stood up and promptly replied:
"They probably went out and sold the second car!"
This somewhat lighthearted reply probably cooled down those present for the pharmacists were also having difficulty to come to terms with the cuts in costs that were being imposed on them.

About this time, I was becoming very disillusioned with the work I was doing and so I decided that the time had come to look for chances further afield, or perhaps even back in Cheshire. So after some discussion with Jean and mindful of the disturbance this might cause I nevertheless gave in my resignation, with no particular thoughts as to what I wanted. I had nothing special in mind so I thought I would find out what answer my old company Boots the Chemists might have to my inquiry. I was invited to attend an interview at Nottingham at which they expressed delight that I might be wishing to re join them. On my return I received a letter offering me an appointment in the East End of London at a salary less than I was getting at present. That didn't seem to fit in with my idea of "new fields" so I turned them down and applied for a post in Northampton. I had an interview with a Mr N--------- who offered me an improved salary and the benefit of a flat over one of his to shops, and so I came to agreement with him to start when my notice had been served out at Loughborough. I was promised a flat over his principal business and I was to manage his other shop about a mile away the other side of the town. This was not quite what I had agreed but left it at that, but I was now informed that the flat would not be ready to use until about a month after I was due to start. So I then went to Northampton ahead of Jean and John and they were to follow a few weeks later. I was to be accommodated in a house nearby which provided as lodgings for about five other "guests" and it proved to be a very comfortable stop gap. The promised flat proved totally unsuitable in that there was a very large lounge on the ground floor to the rear of the shop and all the other rooms were on the first floor which was most inconvenient and even worse the only source of hot water was provided by a gas boiler in the bathroom. This seemed no place for us to relax and enjoy life nor was it at all suitable for a small baby, so it came as no surprise that after a few weeks we agreed that Jean and John should go back to her mother's house in Hoylake whilst I would stay in Northampton and give in my notice,and depart as soon as possible. In addition, the pharmacy itself made work almost quite impossible as I was working until nearly 9 pm each night coping with this new, quite enormous demand for medicines and other supplies. Having complained about all this to my employer, his comment was that it seemed very noticeable that those of us coming out of the services after the war did not really understand how to work, nor did they even want to work! In addition he commented that he would not be employing me further unless I resigned from the RNVR and paid proper attention to satisfying him! His businesses had done very well throughout the war and whilst I did not blame him for that I was not prepared to listen to such bigoted nonsense, and so it can be no surprise that I was on my way shortly afterwards.

In the meantime, Jean and her mother's cousin Alfred Ellison, who ran the family, (or rather assumed that he did) had heard of a newly opened business in one of the estates in Ellesmere Port that had been put up for sale. On my return to Hoylake Alfred Ellison went with me to view this pharmacy which had only been opened six months before After some discussion the owner, who had also a business in Liverpool, asked Alfred:

"In what capacity are you involved in this transaction?"

To which he replied:
"I am the General Factotum of the Family."
I was lost for words. However the morning ended with my agreement to purchase the pharmacy which was to be my own pharmacy and for which I supplied £300 which was all I owned and Jean's Mother supported a loan from the bank in the sum of £2000. This was certainly a new challenge, for the pharmacy was situated in a very poor area and had very few customers and very little stock. As the flat above would not be available for a few months (that sounds a little familiar!) we were invited to stay at Jean's mother's in Hoylake which meant I was obliged to travel daily to Birkenhead by train and then take a bus to Ellesmere Port and this was then followed by a ten minute walk, carefully avoiding some aggressive geese which occupied a large pond close to the bus stop! This made a very long day for me but, happily, two months later, we were able to move into the flat. This was a great deal more convenient and painting and decorating became the order of the day. After we had been there a few weeks, I received a solicitor's letter from Coventry in which Mr Jackson, my former employer, was accusing me of bad management, rudeness to customers, and general dishonesty. This was very disturbing to me and I contacted Alfred Ellison (the general factotum!) who immediately saw that this was a very serious allegation and asked me if there was any truth in these allegations. I replied that they were a great shock and were totally untrue and a total surprise to me. He suggested we put this in the hands of his solicitor who would probably well advise that we engage the services of a barrister, which we did. There then began a lengthy exchange of legal documents of claims and counter claims,

which continued for many weeks and apprehension now took hold of me as to what might be the outcome if it all went wrong. Two days before the case was to be heard in the county Court at Coventry there was a surprise withdrawal of the case and a communication was received from Mr Jackson's Solicitor in the following terms.

"We unreservedly withdraw all and every allegation of mis- management, negligence, incompetence or lack of attention on your part-----------and we admit there never was any foundation for any such allegations or suggestions." and that brought relief and the conclusion of a very disturbed and unhappy event, which had given me many hours of worry even though the accusations bore no foundation. The reason for this attempted outburst will never be known, but I was left with the feeling that that a loss on the Pharmacy was going to be used to adjust some difficulties that might have arisen between Mr Jackson and the Income Tax Authorities. I will say no more except to add that in 1949 signs were beginning to show that the effects on my physical and mental health caused by the strain of the war years, and also this upsetting incident was adding further to the complications which were evolving, as was to be proved later.

CHAPTER TWELVE

Boom Town

Mere wealth can't bring me happiness
Mere wealth can't make me glad
But I'm willing to take a shot
At being rich and sad

- Anon

The somewhat odd title to this chapter will become more apparent as the decade of 1950 to 1960 will reveal and perhaps some explanation is necessary before I proceed. During the war and in subsequent years the Shell Oil refinery at Stanlow, Ellesmere Port had continued to expand. With this had come the rapid development of Ellesmere Port from a small town to a thriving community and in the middle of the decade achieved the status of a borough. The Metropolitan Borough of Ellesmere Port has since continued to develop and is continuing to grow with the ever increasing size of operations at the refinery. This brought about a significant effect on the community and, on reflection; I was pleased to feel that I was part of this challenge.

The year opened with the continuing rationing of food and fuel and power cuts were the order of the day. The business I had now purchased was on one of the working class estates (not my designation!) and it was proving difficult to progress and advance the pharmacy, Deansgate, which was off the long Princess Road and the pharmacy was part of a row of small shops at the far end. The posh title of Deansgate always amused me and always made me think of the centre of Manchester! But this was far from similar. In the early days the local residents were not too sure of who I was and this small anecdote relating an incident went just like this. It was just before closing time when two youths of about 15 years old stood outside and the following conversation took place:

Boy 1: *"You are not going in there are you?"*
Boy 2: *"Why what is wrong with that?"*
Boy 1: *"Well don't forget you have to say please in there"*
Was I beginning to be respected this early?

Whilst on the early days I also had a lady come in and ask me:
"Have you got a toilet roll—my husband has just been in hospital and he has come back with some funny ideas!"
This all augured well and I was beginning to think that I might after all make my mark in this pleasant but tough community.

In the fullness of time the figures for the first year's trading now arrived and showed a turnover of £2784 with a profit of £983 giving me as my first salary the grand sum of £472, which was considerably less than I had been earning in the previous three years. With this came the dawning thought that perhaps this had not been a good idea and that I had once more been directed in a way that I might not had chosen had I been acting solely on my own. However, this was how it was and it was now up to me to make some improvement and face the reality of the situation

Having settled down I now resumed my interest in the Sea Cadets and joined with the Ellesmere Port Unit. The headquarters were in the canal area alongside the Manchester Ship Canal and imagine my surprise when I went to the Headquarters to find that they consisted of the remains of one of my well known dog boats! I never found out which number it had been because the whole of the inside had been gutted and reformed into compartments for drill and instruction. The unit had about fifty cadets and the Commanding Officer had been in charge for most of the war. We blended quite well, but he never forgave me for being a Lieut Commander and senior to him as he was only a Sea Cadet Commissioned Officer. All went well and with a little commonsense and tolerance. I was able to enjoy the work and was most impressed with the enthusiasm and pride with which these boys conducted themselves. Give boys an occupation and interest and pride and good behaviour will most times be the product.

By now the National Health Service was feeling the full effect of unanticipated demands and this was when the Government decided enough was enough and a reappraisal of the funding and contracts was inevitable. This brought immediate reaction from doctors, dentists, pharmacists and the hospital service, which developed, into many angry disputes. Whilst adjustment was inevitable, the manner of the change was not conducive to comfortable relations between the main professions and the Department of Health. This did, however, bring about more organized local action and at this time I joined the new Bebington and Mid Wirral Chemists Association and looking back this must have been the forerunner of my involvement in a greater depth in pharmaceutical affairs which was eventually to have quite an unexpected and dramatic advancement of myself in medical and pharmaceutical management matters both locally and nationally. This local association of chemists functioned very well,and later I became their third chairman, and it was also the source of meeting many pharmacists and making many lasting friends.

Whilst all this was taking place, my health was beginning to show signs that the war years were taking their toll, and the slowness and lack of progress in the business was provided a further contribution. I was acutely aware that I had now the responsibility of a wife and John, now two years old, to look after but my depression grew and grew with the chief manifestation being aches and pains throughout my legs and arms. I later learned that this was what is described as psychosomatic illness where there is a reversal of functions between the brain and the body. This was best described as when a thumb is hit by a hammer the brain and body feel pain, but in the reversal mode the brain produces the reaction and passes pain to the body even though no blow has been received. Things were not good, and all tasks became more complicated for me and after medical consultation it was agreed that the best course was for me to attend a Rehabilitation Centre. The place to which I was sent was called Roffey Park and was situated in Horsham. After a long train journey, I eventually arrived at this beautiful old house with a great spread of gardens extending far beyond the the building. The patients came from many sources, from both service and civilian life. Amongst the “illnesses” were those from the bombing of London, sailors and soldiers and others who had contracted medical illnesses for various reasons, but in all, they were there for illness caused by many forms of stress. There was a daily set routine, the morning was spent in exercises and learning country dancing, which wasn't very exciting or even enlightening, and after lunch with patients then allocated the "washing up"there was now a half an hour rest and then we were sent into the garden and grounds to do tidying up and gardening until 5 pm. Generally it was arranged that you worked with 'someone else' with whom you chatted away the afternoon. It was only after a week or so I realised that these arrangements were carefully planned so the consultants could gain information from patients about other patients when they were next interviewed. This was a sort of (Gestapo) medical spy system and it worked very well and it certainly did no harm and perhaps shortened the rehabilitation time for many patients. Interviews with your consultant were usually held about twice a week, when they made copious notes and I had not a clue as to what they were after. The day ended at 6 pm when we were sent down to the local pub (drinking and smoking was over encouraged) until we returned to base at 8 pm for supper, and then to bed at 9 pm. This must have done me good. and the day came some six weeks later when I became the object of study for all the twelve consultants in a round robin interrogation, and eventually, their final question went as follows: "Was I sure that I was not hiding some problem that I had not told them about?" I replied to the effect that I did not seem to have any more problems than any one of them sitting there! This did not go down very well and I was on my way home the next day.

Returning home I felt very much better but immediately on arrival all the symptoms were back, due I suppose to the return to the environment I had left, but now having been trained how to cope with the problem I gradually became better and better.

Shortly after this John's birthday was approaching and I acquired a small pedal toy for him to which I built on an extension to hold whatever he wanted. I painted this and gave it a number plate and presented it to him on his third birthday. The next day it was gone. Someone locally had spotted it and made it their own, it was never seen again. As I mentioned before, this was a very tough district.

By now I had become an active member of Bebington and Mid Wirral Chemists Association and became their third chairman. It was now felt that representation in the Wirral area of Cheshire was non-existent and along with Eddie Hebron our names were put forward for election to Cheshire County Pharmaceutical Committee. Up to now, there had been no contest and the main representation was in the north east of Cheshire, chiefly the southern area of the Manchester District. When the results were announced, we had topped the poll. On our arrival at the first meeting, held in the Houldsworth Hall in Manchester, we were treated with caution but gradually became established and within a year or so Eddie Hebron became the Chairman and I became the Hon Secretary. We held these positions until 1974 when a total reorganization of the health services took place as will be revealed later.

This was also the year of the Coronation and being a days holiday for all, we all sat round our primitive black and white telly to watch the events throughout the day. Also with us was my brother in law John Ellison and his wife, my sister in law Betty, and half way through the ceremony our set appeared to have gone on the blink. Don't worry said John Ellison it's a fuse. As we had no suitable fuses we were resigned to call it a day. However my brother in law saved the day by producing a "nail!"which he popped in the set and all was well for the rest of the day. A nail indeed! I presumed this remarkable display was the result of his training as a radar mechanic in the Royal Air Force! As the years went by I realised that John although having a Cambridge Degree was absolutely useless at practical things. But at least he saved the Coronation for us

The business was now growing and in 1953 I took over the appointment of a sub post office; which although adding to my earnings was quite a tedious occupation, and always required a couple of hours at home on Sundays to do the weekly balance in readiness for the possible inspection on the Monday morning, which was conducted without notice from time to time. My mother was now living in a flat in Chester and I am afraid I paid all to infrequent visits to see her although she came to Ellesmere Port from time to time. This was also the time of John's first interest in music and it became a ritual for him to listen to Reginald Dixon on the organ in Blackpool Tower Ballroom on Wednesday mornings, not in our flat but with one of our customers who lived in the next street. These small beginnings eventually began the progress to what later became an intense interest in a more classical form, but it was the beginning. The next year John was five and he started to attend the local school which was just 200 yards down the road, this must have been quite an experience for him.

After five years we felt that we would like to live away from the shop, and hopefully aid John's education and so we moved to nearby Little Sutton. This was on a new estate and we purchased a detached house whose design had been used in the Ideal Home Exhibition in London the previous year. This was some place, and was purchased for £4000, which was quite a large sum for a house in 1954. A year before this Jean's mother had died and this money was part of her inheritance. As usual, the whole operation was conducted by Alfred Ellison (the factotum) who seemed to be controlling the distribution of Jean's mother's estate on behalf of the four children, all of whom to my mind, seemed quite capable of conducting their own affairs. After much attention by both Alfred and one of his cohorts (an Liverpool estate agent) the deal was concluded and we moved in. John now went to the small local village school, which had a wonderful environment which was watched over by a superb headmaster. About this time, John started to learn to play the piano and his mentor was this headmaster, Seth Hughes, whom I will always recall with pleasure, for he was an ideal teacher who was always so attentive to his pupils and possibly was the real reason for John's subsequent love of music. Number 10 Sutton Hall gardens was a beautiful house with a large garden opening out to fields at the rear. The house was one of twelve detached houses situated in an oblong cul-de-sac. The twelve families boasted sixteen children ranging from four to fourteen years and most of the time they played well together even organizing a 'school' for themselves The next five years when we lived in Little Sutton were filled with new beginnings. In 1953 I was approached by a Ralph Collin about the forming of an Ellesmere Port Round Table and with about fifteen others we finally received our Charter. This was now the start of a long friendship with Ralph and his family, his early death some ten years later was quite a blow to me, and was the loss of a real friend. My interest in pharmaceutical affairs had now brought me the honour of being Chairman of the Chester Branch of the Pharmaceutical Society and I was delighted to have the company of my mother and my cousin Eleri at the annual Dinner, which was held in the Grosvenor Hotel in Chester. Many happy hours were spent in Round Table activities and the many events, including Children's Outings, on summer weekends when we arranged sports competitions and many other interesting diversions for them

In 1956 when John was eight years old we decided that his education would benefit from the private sector of education and arrangements were made for him to go as a weekly Boarder at Kingsmead School in Hoylake, reference to this School having been provided again by Alfred Ellison (who was on the Board of Governors – of course!). With John's full and enthusiastic agreement he departed on this new adventure, and it seemed to be just what he wanted as it made up for not having any brothers or sisters at that time. On Saturday mornings, he would board the bus at Hoylake and I would meet him by car at Willaston. John did very well at this school and when he was thirteen, he had achieved a good academic record and had won a scholarship to St. Bees School in Cumberland (later known as Cumbria.) We missed him at home but his happiness at the school was adequate compensation.I continued to enjoy the membership of Round Table and somehow or other I found myself on the National Council of Round Tables although my stay in that post was limited by the retiring age of 'Tablers' at the age of 40 years. During my year of office as Chairman of Ellesmere Port Table I persuaded the Members to open, (or more correctly to extend) a new table in Bebington. An Extension Officer called Bert Healing (who had been strongly opposed to this decision!) was elected and over a period of a few months sufficient names had been unearthed to go ahead with arranging for their official affiliation. Bert Healing was just the man for the job as he was a meticulous Customs Officer. At the advent of VAT he resigned his job and became a Consultant in VAT affairs advising many clients (for a Fee) on how to get them maximum accuracy in filing their claims, thus turning from gamekeeper to poacher!

The business at Ellesmere Port had progressed slowly, and it now appeared to me that I had taken it to a point where it would no longer be able to advance any further. A business owned by Walter Taylor in Hoylake had come up for sale, consisting of two pharmacies about 500 yards apart but on opposite sides of the main street known as Market Street. After some soul searching the sale was completed in October 1958. It was a decision that meant we were now obliged to leave our beautiful house in Little Sutton and for the time being, to occupy the flat over the shop at 68 Market Street. The house in Little Sutton was sold for £4000, which was exactly what we had paid for it four years ago and the price is remarkable in that it was the only period when house prices did not inflate. Even though we had now moved to Hoylake John continued as a boarder at Kingsmead School as this was his wish and the progress he was making fully justified the decision. Now that I had the responsibility of three shops the time had come to say goodbye to my opening venture in Ellesmere Port and within a few months, to my relief, I had found a purchaser and this brought to a conclusion the first decade as a pharmacy proprietor.

CHAPTER THIRTEEN

Early Days at Hoylake

You owe it to yourself to be a success,
from then on you owe it to the Inland Revenue.

In mid summer in 1959 we were delighted to learn that Jean had, at last, after many years disappointment and waiting learned that she was pregnant and now early in 1960 we were eagerly waiting the arrival, which was scheduled for some time mid March. At this time, too, my association with Round Table was drawing to a close, the 40-year rule being applied. For the final twelve months, I was elected as a National Councillor of the organization and whilst this sounded good, in fact, proved irksome in that I knew that my time was limited, and so it proved to be. Like many other ex-servicemen, I had enjoyed the fellowship and it was more enhanced by the fact that we knew how to exist together. Later Round Table seemed to attach too much to imagined status in society rather than accepting you for what you were. My final memory of Round Table was listening to the then National Chairman speaking at a dinner when he said *"Let us not be thought of as an organization of 'Do-Gooders.'"* His theme being that the fellowship part was the most important and good works would follow automatically, rather than the other way round. At first I thought that this was a bit "over the top" and a bit too forthright, but on reflection he was so right for I have always felt that the most important thing is friendship and that the will to do good and help others will always spring from it.

On 12th March 1960, Peter was safely delivered and Jean was well which was good. news, and so John now had a brother and his delight at the arrival of him showed in so many ways. In 1961 John had reached the final months at Kingsmead School, had won a fair share of the prizes and had been awarded a scholarship at St Bees School in Cumbria. One of the final events of the summer term was the Swimming Gala and Jean had been selected to present the prizes. So off we went to the open air baths to watch whilst my role on the day was to look after Peter in his pram! It is interesting to recall that this turned out to be one of my last visits to Hoylake Baths as shortly afterwards they were closed and demolished. This marked a period when many of the open air pools became obsolete, or perhaps the next generation couldn't stand cold water! This certainly doesn't fit in with or support the unending dirge of "global warming"!

In the Autumn of 1961 John left Hoylake to become a pupil at St Bees School. The build up to all the attention given by Jean to the filling of his tin trunk so that we could take it to Hoylake Station a few days before his departure. This was called 'Luggage in Advance' and was a system that had no problems and there was never any doubt that the luggage would be there by the time you reached your destination. Modern advances now seem to do just the opposite the luggage may never reach it's destination, maybe never seen again and it is now considered to be a normal event and causes no surprise. It would appear that not all advances in time and education have resulted in improvement. Having dispatched the trunk, a few days later we took John to Exchange Station in Liverpool where, along with other students he traveled up the north west coast calling at many small stations and eventually arriving at St Bees. Since then Exchange Station has disappeared and I surmise that the train journey no longer exists.. This all sounds like the Victorian Era, but it is only about fifty years ago and was at a time when the Railways were modernised under the "Beeching Plan"and disaster has reigned ever since. John soon settled down at St Bees and enjoyed the environment. Each term we would motor to St Bees and take him out for the day. Whilst he was still there I towed my Heron Dinghy up to Bassenthwaite Lake where he was able to go sailing under the guidance of his teachers and on occasions I joined in with them.

The early sixties were the beginning of a five year return to living over the shop and marked the early days of settling down to living in Hoylake and also the early days of Peter's life. As Jean was now managing the pharmacy below our Flat we decided that an "au pair" would be of great help and a few weeks later 'Tilla' a German girl arrived on the doorstep and was duly installed. She proved very capable and friendly but we never really got very close to her and when she left after twelve months being with us we parted on good terms but we never heard from her again. We might have thought that on her return home she would inquire after Peter for a while. But No! We can never understand the German race and I doubt if we ever will or, indeed, whether they will ever understand us.

About this time I purchased a kit to build a "Heron" Dinghy and duly commenced building in the large store room at the back of 63 Market Street (the other pharmacy) and with no previous knowledge or experience worked from day to day (and evenings) to achieve my challenge. This required a lot of thinking and study as each problem came,but in the end it was completed,the measurements checked and recorded by Ken Evans the measuring secretary of Hoylake Sailing Club which I had joined recently, a decision which was to have far reaching effects on my social life for years to come. The new Heron Dinghy No3060 was duly christened TILLA and launched on the lake at West Kirby on Good Friday 1962 in most unpleasant weather, and yet survived its trial run.

About this time we decided to purchase a permanent caravan at Thurstason which was on high ground overlooking the Dee Estuary and with magnificent views across the water to North Wales. This was great fun for Peter and it also took us away from the business over the weekends. It was pleasant to get away, although the packing up on Saturday nights and the return on Sunday nights proved a little tedious for such a short stay. After three years we exchanged this caravan for a smaller mobile one and spent quite a few holidays in North Wales and even a visit to St Bees to visit John near to his School. Eventually after few years caravaning seemed to have lost it's appeal and we sold it off and came back to normal. holidays. Towing a caravan was not my ideal way of relaxing.

Shortly after coming to Hoylake I ended my association with Ellesmere Port Sea Cadets and decided to offer my services to the Wirral Scouting. I was then duly appointed as Group Scout Leader to Hilbre Group of Scouts in Hoylake with the understanding that the term of office should cease when I reached the age of fifty, it being my personal view, rightly or wrongly, that this was an appropriate time to leave a youth organisation and hand over to younger leaders. My eldest son John also became an Assistant Scout Leader and was a useful addition to the team. Peter joined the Cub Scouts who were led by Margaret Ireland as Akela who was also my chief member of my pharmacy staff . During this period I was also a District Scout Leader and latterly Badge Secretary for the District. When I reached the age of fifty I duly relinquished my appointments and was later delighted to learn that I had been awarded "The Chief Scout's Commendation for my services to the movement. At that time I also took into my employ a Senior Scout Peter Nicholson whose career on leaving School had produced difficulties in settling down; but more of Peter Nicholson later.

In 1963 the lease of the shop and flat at 68 Market Street was up for renewal, and after some deliberations and discussions with my auditor, quite contrary to his advice I decided to close down 68 Market Street and combine my operations at The Central Pharmacy, 63 Market Street which was the pharmacy which I personally looked after. This meant that we were now obliged to find living accommodation and on the closure we moved to a flat in Morpeth Road Hoylake. This was not ideal and was considered temporary accommodation until we could find a property to purchase. As Jean was now without employment she decided to offer her services to Hospital Pharmacy and obtained a post at

Victoria Central Hospital. This now proved a significant move for her and she settled down to enjoy a completely different environment and made a great success of her work and later when Arrowe Park Hospital was opened she was transferred into a completely new setting and remained in this appointment until her retirement in 1980, having been totally absorbed in the daily routine of Hospital Pharmacy. It proved to be a good decision. As Jean was now working she engaged a divorced mother and child to live with us to do the housework and prepare the meals. This was quite a shock to me, and I never really approved or accepted this intrusion into my life, but I was well aware it was going to end quite soon. One advantage was that this little girl, her daughter,was a good companion for Peter and they spent many happy hours playing together even if she wasn't as good at playing cowboys and indians as he was!

It was now necessary to empty 68 Market Street and transfer all the stock and fittings down the road to the Central Pharmacy and by pure chance I had just the right helper in Peter Nicholson who was now a full time assistant in my pharmacy. It was quite a novelty to have a male assistant serving all the young girls who came in, but he became a very popular hard worker. Both of us then moved barrow loads of stock and when that was done we turned our attention to the fittings. The first task was remove two large glass carboys (very old antiques) and these being full of most mysterious coloured liquids had to be emptied before they could be moved. The task of sucking on a tube to syphon this off fell to Peter of course. His face as some of the fluid came into his mouth was quite horrific and I wondered if I had poisoned and killed him! However he recovered,but I will always believe that he never forgave me! After unscrewing and dismantling all the fittings we duly took these to my large store at the back of the pharmacy with the promise we would use them to refit my shop later. The decision to close one pharmacy proved to be correct, total stock was reduced and turnover increased to more than the two shops had been turning over together thus proving my initial thoughts that these two shops had been in competition with each other all the time, the two having to be purchased as part of the total sale from Walter Taylor the previous owner.

In the Summer of 1963 we moved to a large semi detached house in Deneshey Road which we purchased for £5100 which then was the going price for such property. Over the last few years I had been increasing my sailing activity. My first crew sailing was with Fred Jones in Falcon No 17 which had been given the name of "Shrike" and my first sail with him was the annual all day Point of Air Race,which unfortunately was abandoned off Hilbre Island as there was now a gale blowing. On the race being abandoned and now that it was low tide we disembarked with all the other crews on to Hoyle Bank which was the sandbank the other side of Hilbre Island, to wait for the next incoming tide to sail back to Hoylake. Unfortunately nobody had told me that I should have brought food and drink for the day's sailing, and so, wet through and shivering I sat on the sandbank for three hours waiting to sail off. Happily I was offered a share of someone's drink and that just about saved a very miserable day. This was the beginning of three very happy years crewing for Fred Jones and it ended abruptly when he died very suddenly, and at a very early age, from a heart attack, but I will always remember sailing at the Straits Regattas with him each year and enjoying the competition with the Falcons from West Kirby Sailing Club.

At this time I was now serving as Hon Treasurer to Hoylake Sailing Club and held this office for some seven years and this enabled me to become acquainted with all the members and remember their names! During this time I served under three Commodores, Frank Jones, Andrew Stratton and Laurie Farrell all this being instrumental in my making many friends in Hoylake and in other sailing clubs. Later I was also invited to join Royal Mersey Yacht Club and, as you will read later, I also served two terms as Treasurer for them. The final part of sailing whilst living in Deneshey Road was sailing with Duggie Upton in Falcon No 7 "Peregrine" Druggie Upton became a great friend, he was not a good racing Skipper, even though he was a retired merchant Navy Captain, but he was enthusiastic and very outspoken! John also sailed with him when he was home from University, and Duggie's sad demise a few years later was a sad end to a most outgoing character. From this you may well surmise that it would appear that I am the kiss of death to my skippers! This could not have been so and with both those two members I was able to share with them many happy hours and experiences.

CHAPTER FOURTEEN

Moving On Again

What we know is not much
what we do not know is immense

- Marquis de Laplace 1749-1827

The five years spent in Deneshey Road were full of incidents and dramatic changes, but I will deal with a lighter side at first. Early in 1964 the Hilbre Group of Scouts combined with the Meols Scout Group to send a party to Switzerland and the Leader from Hilbre Group was John Knowles. If my memory is correct he would be about 19 years old and this was a very big responsibility for him, but along with the Meols Leader this effort was successful. A few weeks later there was a ten day return visit by the Swiss Scouts and we had two of them staying with us. On one of the mornings I took these two sailing in my "Heron" and they enjoyed it so much that they asked could they go again in the afternoon. They were very surprised when I told them this was not possible as there was no water! and as it was very difficult for them to have to understand what tides are and I was obliged to take them to the shore to prove it and they gazed aghast at the miles of sand and no sign of water. We do tend to take things for granted and sometimes do not realise that not all countries have a coastline, and do not even understand what a tide is and why.

John was now attending University in Manchester reading Liberal Sciences,with a particular bent towards Physics. He spent the first year in lodgings in Stockport remarking dourly that even the sparrows had fits of coughing living there! So I can only surmise what it was like for him. To help him I purchased a motorised bicycle for him, I don't think they exist now, and this solved his travelling problems in Manchester, but what the journey was like from Hoylake to Manchester I can only conjecture. With his love of music he was able to gain a Music Scholarship which gave him University "living in" for the next two years, which I am sure proved more satisfactory and more rewarding and gave him more occupation in his leisure hours. Which raises the question do students have "leisure hours"? At the conclusion of his studies and his attaining his BSc Degree he then spent a term at a school at the far end of Deneshey Road at the invitation of the Headmaster who was a friend of mine and obtained his first experience of teaching. At the conclusion Mr Rigby the Headmaster spoke very highly of his work and predicted that John would make a great success in Education, a prediction that has proved to be correct. His music was to prove his principal relaxation as he moved through many appointments both in private and state education. As an aside this school at Hoylake has long ago disappeared and has been replaced by houses, though I really cannot blame my

son for that!. John then moved to Oxford University for his Teacher Training Course and afterwards moved to his first appointment at Mill Hill School on the outskirts of London.

During this time I was still travelling to Manchester with Eddie Hebron attending meetings of the Cheshire County Pharmaceutical Committee. I had now been appointed as Secretary and Eddie was now the Chairman. We held our Meetings in the Houldsworth Hall in Deansgate, Manchester and later in Altrincham and we also contrived to have an Annual Outing to which wives and children were invited. On one of these Sunday outings at Southport I refused to go with Peter on the Big Dipper due to my fear of heights but Eddie Hebron, very much older than I was, having no such problem was delighted to take him, and feeling very humbled all I could do was watch! The work of the Committee was not over demanding and it was very satisfying to be representing all the chemists in Cheshire attending to their various difficulties as they arose. In 1968 I was appointed to a rather unusual and unexpected project by the Runcorn New Town Development Corporation. This organisation had been charged with building a new town on the outskirts of Runcorn to accommodate Liverpool overspill and was conceived with very strict and forward thinking plans and was to be the new home for the many Liverpool families who were still living in poor conditions which was the aftermath of World War II. A team of modern thinking experts formed those bringing this into effect. Amongst many innovations there was to be a special pharmacy supplying the whole new town and it was to provide for the dispensing of prescriptions and the supply of other medical necessities only and there was to be no ancillary trading in this one off pharmacy. This was quite a new innovation and having been brought to the notice of the Royal Pharmaceutical Society they promptly wished to be involved and agreed to the appointment of a pharmacist from Scotland and the Chairman and Secretary of the Cheshire Pharmaceutical Committee, Eddie Hebron and myself. to serve on the Corporation's discussions and ultimately to supervise the tenders for the tenancy of the pharmacy. It was realised that the award of the lease would be an attractive proposition if only because the large numbers of prescriptions it would produce would result in a very lucrative and unusually high turnover. In fact it was commented upon that that whoever obtained the lease would have a "licence to print money!"

After many months of coming and going to Runcorn we eventually reached the point where we were ready to deal with applications for the Lease. There were not many applicants as had been expected, and it was felt that this was because any applicant would need great experience in dealing with this workload and would need a large capital outlay. It was also realised that an applicant of this nature would already be someone with a large pharmacy which they would have to relinquish were they appointed. The criteria were, however,met and an appointment was duly made. The appointed pharmacist stayed about five years and today I have no further information as to the success of the project As a final postscript to this project I would make two comments. Firstly despite the fact that so many experts in various fields having been involved, the problem that was forgotten was that whilst they moved in parents and children they did not provide accommodation for grandparents who being part of the family were often used as babysitters and to provide relaxation for the fathers and mothers and it appeared that this caused many social and medical difficulties. Secondly the rows of blocks of buildings erected were once described as "chicken boxes" and a many years later watching a programme about New Towns I was appalled to see pictures of the Runcorn project in which the town on which so many hopes had been anticipated now looked downcast and appeared to be fast becoming a new slum. Modern brains do not get everything right and our predecessors could still show them a thing or two about desirable housing complexes.

Peter was now at Kingsmead School and although he was making steady progress, things were not going quite as they should be. The problem seemed to be that whilst he appeared exceptionally bright, the pace of teaching was too slow for him and was producing great frustration. In addition, at that time, educationalists had not quite appreciated this problem and tended to treat children like him as stupid and disruptive. Also there never has been a place for a bright child with his peers and this tended to produce bullying and other disturbances. Peter in the final count produced enough good results to win his fair share of rewards and prizes and in addition winning a scholarship to Birkenhead School. Although I will comment on this later, the move to Birkenhead School was a turning point in these problems as the school immediately recognised his talents and arranged to stretch him to the maximum extent and this happily saw the end of what had been a difficult time for Peter, Jean and myself.

Early in 1966 I received a letter from the Clerk to the Cheshire Executive Council advising me that I had been appointed as the Pharmacy Contractors representative on that Council. The Executive Council, based in Chester, was the arm of the NHS that organised the contracts of doctors, dentists and pharmacists throughout the County and amongst other duties held the payroll and dealt with disciplinary matters affecting contractors. Needless to say this entry into NHS organisation matters gave me great satisfaction and pleasure and I remember thinking to myself that at last I had "arrived" and might in time even be Chairman, but little did I realise that this was but a stepping stone to my advancing into many other facets of the health service. For the time being this was to hold a new interest and I looked forward to the monthly meetings and the various sub committees and in addition I had the bonus of making many new friends.

In the course of this service I was appointed to the Cheshire Committee on Drug Abuse. This of course was really at the beginning of what is now a vast and overwhelming problem and the methods used then both by the police and the medical profession have long been outdated. The work consisted of attending the rehabilitation centres and the interviewing of addicts, giving talks and liaising with the police. I must admit I did not always agree with the theories and policies and still feel that using early addicts to lead us to the pushers was wrong because I always maintained that if the "users" were removed from the scene then the sellers and pushers would have no customers. Although the problem is now much larger and more complicated I still hold to my basic theory of removing the customers and then the suppliers of drugs would just go out of business. This may sound unsympathetic to those who fall under the spell of drugs, but I still feel a more positive approach rather than over sympathetic approach would bring us nearer to reality. After all it is the general public who are forced to pay the costs of all this, and they are the real victims of this blight that has beset our country. This appointment terminated after three years being overtaken by larger national intervention, but I will always feel that the early efforts set some of the pattern for the beginning of an appreciation of the gravity of this continuing worldwide problem. My appointment to the Executive Council continued to get more onerous and I seemed to become one of the senior members all too soon but at this time I was not to know that in 1974 there would be the great upheaval of the National Health Service and that my working in Cheshire would cease, the Wirral now being part of the Merseyside conurbation meant a movement in my NHS activities to this new reorganisation.

About this time I had a visit in my pharmacy by a gentleman called Andy McShane,who told me he had been a rating in Coastal Forces and felt we ought to form a Merseyside Branch of CFVA (Coastal Forces Veterans Association) and would I, as a former Officer, assist him in this endeavour. I was a member of the National Association, but I had never thought of meeting local members as feasible or even necessary. I then joined with Andy in searching out possible members and after many months we felt the time had come for an inaugural gathering. It was agreed that I would be their President and the first meeting was called on a Sunday at the Belgravia Hotel in the New Brighton. The Branch was officially opened by Commander Christopher Dreyer RN who was Vice President of the National Association in the presence of the Mayor of Wirral and other local dignitaries. There were about seventy CFVA members and their ladies and the branch got away to a good start. I was not a regular attender and after about two years they moved their meetings to the Liverpool Branch of the RNA. This Branch was well on the other side of Liverpool and for a few years we held regular meetings until 2002 when declining numbers led to the decision not to continue meetings and to close this CFVA Branch. As the years go on the branches throughout the Country are closing as the members grow old or "Cross the Bar". I was not a good attender and frankly found more satisfaction in attending the once a year meeting of the MTB/MGB Officers Association, chiefly because that was where I could meet many friends from long ago. Sadly, again from the natural reduction of attenders, these annual gatherings were discontinued in 2004 and the only link nowadays is the Remembrance Service held for CFVA and the Officers Association at HMS Hornet in Gosport

When it might be thought that 19 Deneshey Road might prove our residence for many years to come, an opportunity occurred in the summer of 1968 to purchase a property on the sea front in Hoylake and having looked at it just once we were left in no doubt that it was just what we wanted.. So for the payment of £7700 (a large sum in1968) we purchased Seaways Cottage in Marine Road and thereby boldly took the risk of pushing up our mortgage fees beyond what we would ever have imagined. Seaways Cottage was a converted Coach house which originally had been part of the estate of

'Breakwater' the large house on the seafront, which was the home of the then General Manager of the former Martins Bank. This gentleman then made his daily journey by his private coach to Birkenhead and then crossing by the Ferry to Liverpool. The Coach House was not on the promenade but on Marine Road which ran parallel with the sea front but about 100 yards further back and nearer the town, and about sixty years ago the Coach House was separated from the main house and this was done in such a way that the separated plot extended right through to the sea front which gave a very large garden and open view of the sea. We soon settled into our new home and have enjoyed the cottage and surroundings ever since, though we have made many alterations inside in keeping with modern requirements. The outside has remained the same with its beautiful white walls and all doors and windows painted black. This certainly proved to be a wise purchase and I was always pleased that I had made an instant decision to purchase the property more so because I learned some time afterwards that I had beaten off some seventeen would-be purchasers.

CHAPTER FIFTEEN

The Seventies

All good people agree
And all good people say
All nice people, like us, are WE
And everyone else is THEY.
But if you cross over the sea
Instead of over the way
You may end up by (if you think of it) looking on WE
As only a sort of THEY!

Early in January 1970 I received a letter from the Clerk for the Peace for the County Palatine of the County of Chester informing me that my name had been put forward for the appointment as a Justice of the Peace. I was very surprised and I have never found out who had put my name forward. Naturally I replied in the affirmative and was duly sworn in at the Castle in Chester the following September. I felt very proud and honoured that I should be asked to serve in this time honoured way of giving service and being in the position to be part of this ancient and timeless British Judicial system. The actual swearing in took place in public in the main Assize Court at the Castle and this was followed by Sherry and Luncheon in the Judges Dining Room. So now I really was a JP! In addition to my local court duties I was also required to sit in twice a year during the Assizes at Chester when they were in session In 1974 this all changed when the Assizes became Crown Courts and the reorganisation of that year linked Wirral with Liverpool and from that time my attendance to Crown Court hearings would be in the old Assize Court in St George's Hall in Liverpool. This was quite an experience and to sit in these famous old Courts, where so many important trials had been held seemed to be all rather unreal at first. The first case in which I sat with a judge, and on retiring with him whilst the jury was out he outlined the possible punishment he would be giving. Imagine his apoplexy when the jury decided the wrongdoer was not guilty! At that moment I wished I had been somewhere else!

On another occasion along with three other magistrates we retired to deliberate and the judge asked each of us in turn what they thought should be done. I was the last to be asked and it went like this:
Judge: *"Well Knowles what do you think should be done?"*
Me: *"I think much the same as the others."*
Judge: *"I didn't ask you that, I asked you what you thought!"*
Judges are not always easy and friendly to be with but I suppose we are really upstarts in their world. This atmosphere of the past suddenly passed into history when the new Crown Court building was completed. It was quite an experience to be sitting in session with a Crown Court Judge and a jury and awaiting the result of their deliberations before the Judge passed sentence, or discharged the prisoner if there was a" not guilty decision" by the jury.

I was attached to the Bromborough Court as part of a team of about forty magistrates, which was smaller than most but by being so it was very friendly and personalised and junior and inexperienced magistrates were often given an early chance to be Chairman of the three magistrates sitting on the case. This did not apply when the larger magistrates Courts were formed by the joining of Birkenhead, Bromborough and Wallasey Courts and where I soon found out that seniority as a magistrate was carefully and jealously protected. I do however have to admit to an early error on my part when I was new to the Bromborough Court. It occurred in a motoring case when the police prosecution had made their case and immediately the defence solicitor claimed there was "no case to answer." At this point the magistrates are obliged to retire and decide whether this is so, and if so, return and give their decision, but when we returned I announced the case "was proved". I should have announced that there was a "case to answer" and then we would hear the defence solicitor. Horror of Horrors, by my announcing that the case was proved instead of saying there was a case to answer, this error of words meant that the motorist must have his case discharged and go free. That was an early lesson for me and reminded me that the principal requirement of a Magistrate is to listen and concentrate all the time.

In 1974 local government and the health service were reorganised and the Borough of Wirral, came into being and as I have mentioned before, and all the various courts became joined and were now classed as Wirral Magistrates Courts with the principal hearings taking place in Birkenhead and Wallasey. This grouped over 160 Magistrates in one list and possibly because there was such a large number there was less personal contact and "seniority" became of more importance, resulting in their being a limited number who could take the chair for the session and greatly diminished the chances of newer Magistrates gaining valuable experience before they would be called upon to automatically take the chair. Cases could fall into about three categories, amusing, serious and sometimes quite uninspiring. Every now and then there would be a small incident which would never be forgotten. I recall a Juvenile Court case where we had five children aged from fourteen down to six years old. It appeared they had all been found in a supermarket at three in the morning and as was usual, they were lined up in front of the bench so that we could talk to them. We were able to do this in the seventies but now they can only be addressed through their "Brief". At this point I asked the six year old if he really was in the supermarket. His instant reply was "No, I was keeping nix outside"! I expect he was praying that one day he could have a younger brother so that he could take a more active part in crime.

Altogether I spent eighteen years as a magistrate and during that time crime seemed to have increased in both severity and numbers. Legislation over those years had been greatly influenced by the advent of the European Union and the Human Rights Laws. But even before then it was often quite difficult to find an appropriate punishment to fit the crime and many was the time when I drove home quite frustrated by the lack of ability to give a suitable and permissible punishment for some of the particularly bad crimes. The demise of the borstal treatment for younger offenders to my mind was a big mistake especially as the soft punishment that followed, meant confinement in better living conditions much more superior homes than at home. I have always hesitated to talk about particular cases and would never give a talk about various cases for I felt they were a matter between myself and the prisoner and should always remain so. Whether social conditions are the cause of most smaller crimes will always be open to debate and I remember one December hearing when a very small boy appeared before us and having been persuaded to take his overcoat off whilst in court, he did so and stood there in nothing but a vest and "wellies". The Inspector present remarked afterwards that he thought these poor little mites were inevitably bound to be criminals from the "moment of conception" It's a very sad and sobering thought to which, even today, no one seems able to produce a suitable answer to this unending problem, now unhappily continuing to increase.

There were, of course, some lighter moments. One Monday morning a bedraggled female "wino" came before me having spent the night in cells having been found to be drunk and disorderly the previous night. Even then she managed to be missing when her case was called and when she appeared, her solicitor (a very well known senior Birkenhead solicitor) asked her:

"Why were you late in appearing before this Court?"

She replied, *"I have just married Barry Manilow and he is waiting for me in his car outside."*

Solicitor: *"Then you had better get down below and get a Fiver off him because Mr Knowles is going to fine you for being late."*

Quite naturally this case dragged on and a now very impatient Solicitor said:

"You do realise you are before this bench for being drunk and disorderly?"

She then replied: *"Pouff talk about the pot calling the kettle black!"*

The case did eventually come to an end but it had enlivened a Monday morning.

Many years have passed since that incident and I suppose I could relate many similar incidents. The work embraced mainly three kinds of courts, the Criminal one, the Juvenile Court, and the Domestic Panel. The latter panel was a cross section of the trials and troubles of life and matrimonial disagreements. There always seemed to be sympathy for both sides and it appeared that so many of these cases sprang from stress and financial difficulties. The willingness of these couples to find a way through their troubles was often most encouraging and sometimes the doubt and and distress is not always helped by their solicitors who sometimes seem to sow ideas into their clients heads which do not always help resolution of their case. One of the highlights of the domestic courts was dealing with the adoption of children. The child was always present and the joy expressed by both the child and that of the prospective parents was a joy to behold and always made the morning so worthwhile.

Eventually the time came when I was no longer entitled to serve and I was transferred to the Supplemental List of Commissioners of the Peace and duly received this appointment from the Duchy of Lancaster's Office. This was not very active appointment and the powers held are nominal, but it does allow the continuance of the title Justice of the Peace to be used, which I think is right and an honour which has been proudly held. On leaving I had a number of letters from other magistrates and I quote from two: "Good magistrates of your excellent calibre are very short on the ground and the valuable experience you were able to give us less knowledgeable colleagues will long be remembered by many" and from another colleague "You will be greatly missed by all your colleagues but especially by members of the domestic panel and I would like to express my personal thanks for your quiet and solid support since I been Chairman."

These are but two quotes from the many letters I received and it does no harm to realise that your services have been noted and appreciated by your colleagues and helps to confirm that the many hours of service have been a worthwhile contribution to life in the Wirral. Whether I was a good magistrate was for others to judge, but what is most important is that I have been able to make a contribution to the continuation of the time honoured service of justice in the United Kingdom which has stood the test of time, but which is now being endangered by certain politicians under the guise of progress. Now more than ever there is need for stability and the trial of people by their peers has long stood the test of time.

The following year 1971 I received a letter from the Chairman of the Directors of Hoylake Sailing Club advising me that they had co-opted me as a Director of the Company and this would be ratified at the next AGM. Naturally I was very delighted and very surprised for it was unusual to appoint a Director who was not a past Commodore, in fact the only other one was George Stratton who served as Official Starter for many many years, and following his sudden death I was now being asked to fill the vacant place Previously I had served as Hon. Treasurer for seven years and assumed this must have influenced the decision to invite me to join the Board. It was quite unusual for a Sailing Club to be a Limited Company and the reason that this course was decided upon is well documented and was the result of the Club having an over profligate Commodore!. It would appear there had been many disputes and resignations and the problem was solved by forming the Company about 95 years ago and this has worked very well ever since. Six Directors were appointed and they delegated the management of the day to day working to the Flag Officers and a General Committee. As I write this, in the years 2009 I have therefore been a director for some 39 Years with the exception of the two Years 1997 and 1998 when I served as Commodore. Over all this a period of time, I was for many years Chairman of the Company, but after my two years as Commodore I returned and did not go back as Chairman. During my term as Chairman I felt that the procedure at the Annual General Meeting was not correct in that there was no separate Company Meeting so the arrangements were altered and the Company Meeting was now to held first and then the Club Meeting Chaired by the Commodore was held.. This now rectified matters legally and seems to work very well. During the long period of service as a director there have been many changes of personnel on the board and this has always been of added interest and, more importantly, has been to the advantage of the Club.

In 1971 came further surprise, as if I hadn't had enough since the turn of the decade, for I now received a letter from the Royal Pharmaceutical Society indicating that I had been Designated as a "Fellow" of the Society. This was a great professional honour as these awards are limited to a few each year and as the decision is made by a panel of Fellows and to be elected by ones professional peers is quite unique. Being a Fellow does not mean onerous duties, but is just a recognition of the efforts made to further the profession and was probably motivated by my work for pharmacists in Cheshire and the Runcorn Development operation. Unfortunately with it came jealousies as the implication was that I had become "One of them",whoever "them" were. To this day I have no idea who recommended my name for this honour, but the fact that it was felt by others that I was a worthy recipient was very pleasant to note. Whilst all this was going on my work on the Cheshire Executive Council was increasing and in mid July 1971 I found myself attending an Executive Council's Conference in Brighton. With me was The Clerk to the Cheshire Executive Council (Fred Hayter) and whilst taking a stroll along the sea front he asked me if I would be interested in being one of the two North West Representatives on the Joint Pricing Committee for England and Wales. This was the body that organised the pricing of the NHS Prescriptions submitted by all the Chemist Contractors and I replied that I would be interested and left it at that. I had completely forgotten about this until I received a letter from the National Executive Councils Association advising me that I had been elected to one of the North West places. The organisation of this election lies with the Clerk's to the various Executive Councils and the power game takes over. Obviously my Clerk had been able to gather the right number of votes for me. This marked the start of my being involved in a broader scene other than local health matters. This was to be the beginning of many years of being involved in prescription pricing matters and a few months later I attended my first meeting which was held at the old Headquarters of the Royal Pharmaceutical Society in Bloomsbury Square in London. The Chairman was James Anderson-Stewart who was a pharmacist of considerable experience and reputation. The Committee was divided into four groups and I was seconded to the Equipment and Premises group. There was something very "old World" about the way this body worked and before leaving members were even presented with a slip of paper advising them of the times of their train home! The numbers of prescription forms being processed were rapidly increasing and the organisation was hard put to keep up with the workload. After the first year I found myself appointed Vice Chairman and this rapid promotion still remains a mystery the only reason I can find was that I was a pharmacist which seemed to be appropriate as the majority of the sixteen members were not so, being from other walks of life. I was able to learn about the work and the skills of Chairing Committees from Anderson Stewart and I will always be grateful for his patience and the quite strict discipline he expected, and he was the first of the few who gave me so much of their experience and guidance over many years in the in the different organisations to which I became involved. Just when I seemed to be settling in to this work the whole of the NHS and Local Government was totally reorganised. This was the great upheaval of 1974.

I doubt there had ever been such an upheaval in the British Isles as that which took place in 1974 which saw the changes in county boundaries, long standing county names disappearing, local boroughs being absorbed, and a total change in the way the National Health Service was to be organised. Hoylake was detached from Cheshire now becoming part of the Borough of Wirral and grouped in the postal area of Liverpool. This was far from well received by the Wirral population who had historically always been associated with Cheshire. Many hospital groups just disappeared and in their place came the Regional Health Authorities and these in turn became responsible for a number of Area Health Authorities. Because of these changes all my various appointments connected with Cheshire ceased to exist and in their place I received a surprise in being appointed to Wirral Area Health Authority and added to this a place on the new Family Practitioner Committee, the successor to the Executive Councils and finally to Wirral Chemists Contractors Committee which was the equivalent of the Cheshire Pharmaceutical Committee,which as may be recalled was the start of this "journey" in public service. The Joint Pricing Committee now became the Prescription Pricing Authority, elections were held, and I retained my position as Vice Chairman. All this had taken place, with all it's various upheavals after many months of work before the appointed day and caused a lot of heartache to those who were being left behind. The rights and wrongs of this upheaval can never be debated, because once implemented there was no turning back, but sadly it saw the demise of historical names and places which had endured through the many centuries of our existence and history.

CHAPTER SIXTEEN

The Revolution in the Pricing of Prescriptions

Courage is what it takes to stand up and speak,
Courage is also what it takes to be silent.

- Winston Churchill

Two years after the reorganisation of the Prescription Pricing Authority the Department of Health commissioned a Professor Tricker, attached to Oxford University, to conduct a detailed study of the pricing arrangements with a particular instruction to consider the pricing of the prescriptions with the aid of computers. At this point in time this was a subject of great agitation and disruption by the Administrative & Clerical Unions who kept on referring to these new machines as "New Technology" and were very opposed to its introduction as they believed it would mean loss of jobs. The purpose of this research was not only to test the feasibility of capturing the data, but to use that wealth of information to analyse doctor's prescribing and hopefully control the now escalating costs of drugs in the health service.

The Tricker Report was immediately accepted as the way forward and the first move was the reconstitution of the authority members to meet the oncoming challenge. The new members represented a wide range of those who would be involved and consisted of four pharmacists representing the Pharmaceutical Services Negotiating Committee, three doctors representing the General Medical Services, four Family Practitioner Committee Members, a University General Practice Professor, a representative of the Department of Health and a representative of the Community Health Councils. I felt very fortunate to be one of the pharmacist members, having been appointed by the Pharmaceutical Services Negotiating Committee and thus retained "my place" The final change was that the Chairmanship would now be a lay person appointed by the Minister of Health. This appointment of the Chairman, when it was announced caused quite a raising of eyebrows, but it proved to be a stoke of genius. Geoffrey Dinsley was the then General Secretary of the Newcastle Co-operative Laundries, who not only dealt with the whole of the miners clothing and laundry, throughout Tyneside but they had also developed a thriving computer service,and were well ahead of similar competitors. The Pharmaceutical Journal for the following week headlined the appointment with the words "Laundryman to run the pricing of prescriptions". which may have caused some amusement and perhaps even concern, but proved to be quite the wrong description of his capabilities. Geoffrey proved a most capable and knowledgeable Chairman and was instrumental in the eventual success of the target he had been set. At the first Meeting I was appointed his Vice Chairman and this was the beginning of our serving together for nineteen years. It was also the beginning of a great understanding of each other and resulted in a very personal friendship which lasts to this day The Chairman immediately appointed me to Chair the Finance and General Purposes Committee dealing with all the staffing and finance matters. Once having done so he never sought to interfere, in fact he also sat on my monthly management meetings. which were held in London and I will always remember him saying "you get on with that and I'll get on with the computerisation!" This sounded rather simple but it gave the base for our working together. Now and then he might rap my knuckles but it was always in the best of spirit. It grew into a wonderful understanding and I believe we were a complete match for each other.

What Geoffrey had omitted to tell me was that my appointment carried with it the Chairmanship of the Joint Industrial Relations Committee. This was the stormy ground with the unions, mostly on staffing and pay, but the big cloud gathering was to complete the negotiations with the onset of the forthcoming computerisation which was to involve retraining of all the staff of over 2000. It proved to be a long and patient haul which in the end was satisfactorily resolved, and happily everyone involved obtained the benefit of improved working conditions and also without any redundancies, which was a great surprise to the two Unions involved. The Pricing Authority, which was called a Special Health Authority consisted of Eleven Divisions, which is what the eleven offices were called and apart from the Division at Newcastle the ten other Divisions were spread over Tyneside, Yorkshire and Lancashire and had been the result of government diversion of employment to the north in order to ease unemployment in the 1930's Depression. The Head Office was in Newcastle, but the work involved visits to all these outposts during the year and many of the meetings with the unions were held in one or other of them.

The headquarters also contained the administrative staff and they, and the pricers, were mostly female employees. It took me at least a year to understand fully the "Geordie" accent but these girls (ladies) were the salt of the earth and I soon came to understand them.

I will never forget my first visit to Newcastle when I opted to go by train. The journey took about four hours passing through Manchester Leeds, Darlington, Durham and finally Newcastle. By then I was very hungry as I had not realised that there were no buffet cars on the cross country journeys. Eventually I arrived just in time for the meeting and then raced to get the five o'clock train to Liverpool, and again no food! Never again! I then decided that it was best to go by car and on closing my pharmacy at Hoylake at 6 pm I would drive north up to Teebay and spend the night there, afterwards crossing Shap Fell in the early hours of the next day and so on into Newcastle. At the end of the day I would leave about 5 pm and have a leisurely drive back to Hoylake. This proved to be the pattern for the many years that followed As a little diversion from this discourse there was a small but amusing incident which occurred when my Brother Alun was acting as locum manager at the Newcastle Branch of the National Westminster Bank and on arriving one morning walked into the Managers Office only to find that there on a very tidy desk lay a single piece of paper for his attention. This was a Transfer Draft for Two Million Pounds signed by me on behalf of the Authority. This was the monthly wages and expenses transfer and my brother just could not believe that the signature was that of his "little" brother! He just could not believe it but in the end was obliged to admit that Geoff, had perhaps, got on in the world without him noticing it!

Over the nineteen years spent in this appointment many of the staff who were juniors in my early days were later experienced enough to be applying for the top Pricer. Positions. One of these who was now very well known to me came before a promotion panel of which I was in the Chair, and on sitting down in front of my desk she said:
"Oh, Mr Knowles, if I had known I was coming before you I would have put on a longer skirt."
This liberty taken did not in any way prevent the promotion of a very attractive and forthcoming lady whose vivacious nature was well known to all.

Now just a word about the Unions and staff side committees. The Two Unions involved were NALGO now renamed UNISON and the smaller one was ANHSO (National Association of Health Service Officers. In the main many difficult matters were reasonably resolved most of the time but NALGO always wanted to throw it's weight about. I soon learned how the game was played and with caution and patience things moved along quite smoothly. NALGO were always led by one of their professional employees who always wanted to try and establish his power base whereas ANSHO were more amenable and one of my "perks" was to attend and address ANHSO's Annual Conference each year. One year when this was held in Blackpool produced an amusing incident the likes of which really only appear in joke books. The Mayor of Blackpool that year was a small effervescent lady accompanied, as you may guess, by a very large husband, and having dined and wined well she made a very good (if garrulous) speech of welcome. The very dashing young chairman rose to reply but he was continually harassed by the mayor who would not stop talking. A very patient chairman, having borne it for so long, then removed his handkerchief from his top pocket opened it and placed it over the head of the mayor saying:

"That's what we do to my Budgie when he wont shut up!"

It went down very well, and principally with the husband of the mayor.

During this time I was also informed that I had been appointed to the Whitley Council for Administration and Clerical Staff which was the national body dealing with wages agreements and staffing arrangements for the whole of the British Isles. When attending my first meeting of this illustrious body the principal Officer from the Health Department suggested I might like to join him for lunch. It appeared he had a flat nearby and so I went with him and was regaled with cheese and biscuits and a very tolerable red wine. During this time I was asked many questions chiefly about the Chief Officer at Newcastle. I later realised it was not as kind an invitation as it appeared, it was in effect, a crude information gathering session. I still had a lot to learn! The work on Whitley Council proved to be very demanding especially as we were negotiating on annual pay awards of up to 15% at that time due to the extraordinary advance of inflation. This was quite an unreal situation and hopefully now long passed never to return again. The early advent of the computer with its new technology brought quite unusual problems, and I recall an occasion when at a meeting of

the management side when consideration was being given to upgrading the scale of the computer operators in the Regional Health Authorities. It appeared that there was only one operator to each region and so it would not be too expensive and would be appropriate. I then informed those present that in my authority I had just over 2000 operators who would benefit. This caused consternation. I was totally wrong according to them and belief only came to them when I invited six of them to come to Newcastle and see for themselves. They did, and then they believed, and I think the alteration was then delayed, but not for long. The effect on the Staff at Newcastle and our other Divisions and the unions were somewhat difficult, but I listened patiently and I do recall at one meeting the NALGO representative said:
"You haven't said anything yet Mr Knowles."
To which I replied:
'Why ? Is my silence bothering you?"

It seems that when I am quiet at these meetings the other side just don't know why. But I did and it was comforting to know I had them worrying. In the end when final agreement was reached the consensus opinion after about a years working was that the pricers were quite pleased at the change and bigger outputs meant bigger bonuses. I enjoyed the cut and thrust both in London and with the unions in Newcastle and when my term of office with the PPA was terminated I was invited to a farewell luncheon in Newcastle by the two unions I had been involved with, which I took as a great compliment and recognition of their appreciation of my working with then. The pricing authority did not show their appreciation in quite this way!

The first division to be computerised was at headquarters at Newcastle, and in preparation for this an additional floor of that section had to be constructed to raise a platform three feet above the existing floor to accommodate the wiring and special temperature controllers. In addition to bring the equipment into the building a scaffolding had to be erected, a window taken out, and all of this was very much in contrast to the installation in the eleventh division some ten years later when all the equipment was carried in by hand and no other alterations had to be made. This indicated the rapid advance in computer equipment and technology in those few years and any new replacements are now even more compact and require less room. In all of this discourse I do not seem to have covered the purpose behind all this activity and I think the best way is for me to give an abstract from a talk entitled "PPA leaves the quill pen age behind" which I gave to the Institute of Pharmacy Management when they visited Newcastle during one of their Annual Conferences which in this instance was held in nearby Durham:

"The introduction of a computer system for the processing of prescriptions had proved an immense task, but it meant that The Prescription Pricing Authority had left the "quill pen age" behind and that an increased prescription intake in the last two years (1987/1988) had been compensated for by a significant increase in the PPA's efficiency. In 1980/81 the PPA employed some 2050 full-time staff and handled some 322 million prescriptions. In the current year (1988),a reduced number of staff (1750) was able to handle some 360 million. This increase in output had been achieved whilst maintaining previous standards of overall efficiency.

It was difficult to forecast the level at which output would stabilise, but estimates were that the number of prescriptions processed would grow from the present 360 million to 380 million by 1990, followed by even greater numbers as each year passed.

The PPA which was part of the National Health Service had two functions, checking and the pricing of prescriptions, and providing information on drug usage to the department of Health and to Doctors. The work was carried out by staff in eleven different centres in the north of England. These 11 divisions processed the prescriptions from forms sent in by 11000 pharmacy contractors and 24000 doctors throughout England, and it is believed that the PPA represented the largest data-capture in the United Kingdom and probably even in Europe. Processing prescriptions was a skilled clerical task. There were about 17,000 different medicines, which were available in various pack sizes, so the system covered a total of 87,000 different coded items. Staff had to read difficult handwriting and apply complex payment rules, deciding whether what the doctor prescribed was actually dispensed and whether the dispensing was acceptable. Staff had to look out for unusual items, possible forgeries, stolen prescriptions and suspected irregularity. There were up to 61 points on a prescription of which staff had to be aware.

On average one prescription was keyed in every 14 seconds. Approximately nine seconds were spent in examination and interpretation and five seconds for keying. The sheer volume of prescriptions meant that one extra keystroke could cost an extra £250,000 on a yearly wage bill of £15 million. Computerisation of the PPA's operations had been a direct result of the recommendations of the Tricker report of 1977 which was based on a government initiated inquiry into the functions, organisation and constitution of the authority. The first division had gone "live" on the new computer system in August 1983 with computerisation of pharmacists prescriptions completed by September 1986."

It must be noted that the figures given will now have altered and increased with the passage of time and the authority has again been re-modelled to meet the challenge."

So ended nineteen years of most interesting work and wonderful experiences...

CHAPTER SEVENTEEN

Getting Into Perspective

But I have so little done
So much to do.
- Alexander Graham Bell

The appointments in 1970 continued to arrive, as you will read later, but at this stage I feel I must indicate that my main purpose of earning a living for my family and myself was not dominated by outside voluntary diversions. Apart from the Pricing Authority the other appointments were local and would never occupy more than a half day and sometimes much less than that. To compensate for this diversion of my time I was fortunate in finding (at different times) two lady pharmacists who were able to cope with my unusual and often unplanned calls upon them. In order to keep well in touch with the main objective, I now started to go to work at 7 am daily and in the two hours before opening dealt with all the routine work. In addition my senior assistant, Margaret Ireland, also came to work at about 8 am (by her own choice) and this enabled all the routine matters, ordering and stock sorting well ahead of opening hours. Both the part time pharmacists became very much part of the business and it certainly gave them a more positive interest. In addition my service on these many organisation was also a learning curve in management experience and finance matters.

I was therefore able to look at my own business from outside and not being too near to the "coal face" gave me a better perspective and subsequently proved to work to the advantage and advancement of my business I had long ago realised that the pharmacy would reach a point where it could advance no more and my main objective was to increase efficiency and thereby get the maximum return for my investment. The investment available was the limit of my capital and by now I had reached a calmer period when dreamy ambitions had to be tempered with reality. I did not listen to those who always wondered why I did not buy a larger pharmacy, say in Liverpool, but it became obvious to me that, with even a turnover twice of that of my Hoylake pharmacy, by the time I had paid all the extra rents and expenses, and in addition to perhaps two hours a day travelling the result was likely to be no greater than operating in quiet Hoylake and enjoying more hours of freedom, and sharing in the village life.

Peter Nicholson continued to work for me (my one and only male assistant!) but after about a year he asked if I could get him into one of the Liverpool chemist wholesalers. I seemed to have the right contact and he then moved to Ayrton Saunders in the department which supplied chemists with their prescription requirements. He was able to tell me that the experience gained working for me was proving of great help and value. He progressed rapidly, but after a few years he moved again to "Rowlands of Wrexham" taking the post as manager of the ethics supplies. Suffice it to say he proved to be excellent at his job and after many years became a director of the company eventually being able to retire at quite an early age with a very satisfactory pension. So the boy I picked up out of the wilderness, and made good has always filled me with the satisfaction that I was instrumental in being part of the route to that success. One O level in English therefore proved not to be the recipe for disaster.

It would appear that this chapter will pay no attention to the passage of time and will just be a commentary on my daily life and general happenings. I say this because most of the other chapters concern themselves with specific appointments, whereas this one talks about my life, my home, and my family. I think what needs to be said is that although Jean and I led a comfortable life we nevertheless were always cautious with how we spent the earnings of the business and the salary she was earning in the hospital service. Although we had an agreed decision that John and later Peter should have the best educational start in life this nevertheless required postponing a more lavish life until later. This certainly was not a burden and this was well rewarded by the success of their attainments and the subsequent way their lifestyle developed. Perhaps it is not appreciated that owning a business presented many problems and the till was not a sort of piggy bank as a lot of people would tell you! To progress and expand a business it must be supplied with capital, and the only source available to me would have to come from any profits made, and it follows that personal income from the business then becomes restricted It is quite interesting to note that although I had a small loan from the bank at the start this was never fully paid off until the last three years before I retired. However there was a continual problem in that inflation meant that the cost of stock purchases were always rising and therefore the replacement of stock was a considerable call on capital, and as inflation was at one time as high as 15% this was an ever increasing problem in that our annual return from the business was continually restricted. However the spin-off from this came when I retired, sold the pharmacy, and the stock turned into cash in my bank.

I have dwelt with this, as I always felt this had effect on our ability to perhaps give more financial help to the boys during their university years. I can imagine they will both be very cross when they read this and at no time did they ever indicate or indeed need help and modestly this just might have been the good example set by their parents teachings about life in general. I am sorry to write this little discourse, but I suppose all parents will always think they could have done better. On the positive side their mother always saw that they were properly equipped to deal with life and I was proved quite wrong for Peter, when at Cambridge, was able to purchase a new bicycle and an engagement ring without any call upon us!

When we settled down in Seaways Cottage we were able to enjoy every minute of the lovely garden and the daily outlook of the sea. Both the boys sailed with Hoylake Sailing Club and John of course was able to get the benefit of the dinghy I had built for I was able to take it to Bassenthwaite Lake for him to join in the sailing during term time whilst at St Bees School. Being at home Peter was much more involved and was able to take advantage of the opportunity to sail in my

Opera Class "Fidelio" with Peter Bryson with whom I had done a deal to take Peter sailing after I was no longer able to sail as my leg injuries had worsened. He therefore was sailing in Operas when he was only twelve and he was taught so much by his "Skipper." This proved of great advantage when he went to Cambridge and he soon found himself in the University Sailing Team. At first, when I heard this, I was delighted but second thoughts came into my head that this might affect his studies, but I was wrong (once again) for after the first year he worked hard at his studies, gave up the sailing, and whilst working very hard and with great success also found the love of his life who a few years later was to become Mrs Phillipa Knowles.

The main object of this chapter has been to indicate in some way that the preceding ones and the ones to come must not be taken out of context, and to skip through the family and daily life to tell it in full would take another book. Therefore I must skip through highlights so that the main thrust of my writings in this book only represent a relatively small amount of my total life and must be viewed as such. I must admit that a very large part of these years were spent in my pharmacy both in and out of opening hours. I suppose this must be the accountancy streak that runs through my family for I spent many hours pondering over figures and trying to improve my business acumen. What really was at the base of this was that I was under capitalised throughout the whole of my business life and whilst I never did exceed my loan limits it was always depressing that my month end Balance Statement always showed me to be "in the red". In addition to this there was also the wholesalers bills and they were very patient with the credit they allowed pharmacists in general, bearing in mind that from day one the NHS were always seven weeks behind in their payments and that these amounts were growing larger all the time as the prices and numbers were continually rising. On reflection I suppose I occupied too much time worrying when deep down inside me I knew that I always hated and still do, being in debt of any sort. Not a bad trait I suppose. Happily, as I mentioned earlier, the day did arrive when I was in credit, but it had taken a long time. The learning process, from all these activities was of great assistance in finally reaching my objectives.

At this time the boys were growing up and starting on their careers. We spent many happy caravan holidays with the Ellison Family and when they moved to Wroxham many pleasant times were spent sailing on the Norfolk Broads. In all these there were many incidents and that period of time left many memories for both families including joint

Christmas day celebrations. After a few years John became engaged and married Roey, they had met at the Annual CSSM Holiday camps to which they gave great service. There was always the joke about CSSM which was said to stand for "Come Single Soon Married", and so it proved to be. As the years went by my three grandaughters arrived (not all at the same time!) and they spent many happy hours with us enjoying the seaside and our garden. Like most families little girls have their moments of discord and I remember Hannah (the eldest) running to me saying Louise had bitten her. I told her to go back and bite Louise which she did! End of quarrel. These moments move on rapidly and two are now married and Amy, the third one, about to be, in the Spring of 2009. Unfortunately we have not seen as much of Peter and Phillipa's children, the main reason being geographical, but we keep well in touch. This also reminds me that when Peter was about to go to Cambridge we gave him a stock of two shilling pieces (yes, it was that long ago) with instructions to phone us at 9 pm every Sunday night, which he did—and still does most Sunday nights now, but not with the same two shilling piece stockpile. Jean and I shared 43 years together in Seaways Cottage and in the latter years we felt the garden was becoming too big a task, so we agreed to sell off the front half and this took away our wonderful sea view. There have been no regrets and the Cottage is now very well protected from the all too frequent south westerly winds.

There is so much of my life that has been spent here in Hoylake and as the years have moved on, many friends are no longer with me, but happily there are so many new ones and new activities in social life that keep filling the many many years. Jean passed away in 2003, we had however celebrated our Golden Wedding with all the family in 1995 and had shared many happy and sometimes difficult hours together. After a year and a half on my own I then married Colleen who though many years younger than me has brought the sharing of a new life, new friends and this has certainly given me the chance to spend a few more happy years (maybe more than a few) and enjoy new and continuing activities rather than being confined to a nursing home which might well have happened.

From this you will see that the majority of my life has been full of interests and the narrative of this book does not seek to show them all but merely to show that despite the many honours and appointments they represent a relatively small total in hours occupied by them compared with my professional and family life lived here in Hoylake, Ellesmere Port and other places before that.

CHAPTER EIGHTEEN

Hospitals and Health

Good planning and organisation are just crutches for those who cannot handle stress and caffeine!

Everything is costed and nothing valued

By the end of 1973 I felt that the seventies had been full of so many events in my life that nothing else could possibly happen. Wrong again! For at the end of that year I was informed that I had been made a Fellow of the Institute of Pharmacy Management International. I had been an active member for some time of this new pharmaceutical organisation that was, at last, going to study the needs of good management in the profession. After a number of years as a member it became my turn to be their Chairman and it then fell to me to Chair two of their Conferences one in Kinsale in Ireland and the other in Aldeburgh in Suffolk. The latter one included a visit for a concert at the Maltings which place was the creation of the composer Benjamin Brittain.The former one in Kinsale was remembered by two things. Firstly the argument with the President who felt we should only Toast the Queen whilst protocol demanded that we toast the President of the Republic as well. Eventually we elected for peace and did justice to both countries. The second event took place at the interval of the dinner before the toasts when we found that on returning to our places everyone's drinks had been cleared away! The lady manager duly apologised and replaced all the drinks at no cost. Life plays funny tricks for when in my second year and the Conference was at Aldeburgh the manager of the Hotel was the same one that we had encountered in Kinsale! The drinks were safe this time. Later I was for nine years their General Secretary and this was followed by my being made one of their Vice Presidents. This new body did not always appeal to the "Society", but over many years has been accepted and a great deal of the principles have now been integrated in the University Pharmacy MSc course studies.

This was nothing compared with my surprise a few weeks later when I received a letter from the Chairman of the new Regional Health Authority informing me that I had been appointed a member of Wirral Area Health Authority. This seemed most unusual for a pharmacist to find himself in this position, but I must add this was a personal appointment and not a representative one. How this came about I will never know, or ever find out who had put my name forward, but obviously for some reason I had been felt to be suitable. This was now going to open up for me a new world of hospitals and health services in general and was going to require a large learning curve from me. The Chairman of this Authority was William Whitelaw whom I knew quite well as a senior magistrate attached to the Bromborough Court. I felt it was a very wise choice and he was very knowledgeable in Hospital matters, having been Chairman of Clatterbridge Hospital under the old regime. I do recall when making a Hospital visit, him saying to me *"You know, Geoffrey, I am not a believer but I do envy people like yourself who have a faith to guide them and I always feel there is something missing in my life".* I always felt that this was a remarkable and honest statement coming from a man who had given so much of his time to helping others in so many ways. During the next three years I was able to learn so much from his example.

I was now about to serve with fellow members from many walks in life, medical and dental consultants, nurses, local councillors and other lay members, many representing experience in other walks of life and the first task was to get to know each other and so become a team. To achieve this we were sent to Leeds University for a week to be indoctrinated into the new Health Service provision and appreciation of the tasks before us in bringing this about and making it work. On our return we were next involved in "appointments" because all the officers positions were now up for filling and the applicants were mostly those who had similar appointments either on the Wirral or in the Region and this was therefore very time consuming and even bordering on unreality. Many senior officers took this opportunity to retire (which they were allowed to do) and this afterwards resulted in the loss of great experience and the rapid promotion of lower ranks, which perhaps on balance about justified itself.

Amongst my early duties were the tasks of monthly visits to the Concourse at West Kirby to note the progress being made on the provision for a Health Centre within the building and to comment on the layout of the doctor's surgeries and the administration working areas. This seemed an awful waste of time but I suppose it was part of a learning curve. In addition I was also given the position of attending the progress of the building of Arrowe Park Hospital which at that time was half way through the construction. This new hospital had been designed to replace all the hospitals in Birkenhead, but with the 1974 reorganisation it was now scheduled to be a Wirral Area Hospital and the reduction in Birkenhead Hospitals was to be modified. The scheme now included the closure of small hospitals and nursing homes throughout Wirral and the arrangements for this were vested in a strategy group of five Authority members and in which I found myself included. Someone must have faith in me somewhere! This did not apply to the Pharmacy Contractors Committees throughout Wirral who for some reason seemed jealous of my appointment, whereas my view was that they were very fortunate to have a voice for their problems, even if I was not appointed for that purpose. There then followed hospital visits, various different Committee meetings, and tribunals either for promotions or for disciplinary matters. The first three years passed very quickly, and happily I received a further appointment for another three years. Mr William Whiteside now retired as Chairman having steered this new body with great skill.

The newly appointed Chairman (or should I say Chairperson!) was a Mrs Phyllis Roberts who came with a formidable reputation. I did not know of her before this but she had been the Agent for the Labour Member of Parliament for Birkenhead and after that a powerful Labour member of Birkenhead Council. On receiving this appointment she completely divorced herself from politics and in doing so took a lot of abuse from her Labour and Trade Union associates. I was amazed at her strength of character in doing this and she proved to be a superb leader of our hospitals, whilst always retaining the love and affection of all the Birkenhead people who knew her especially when visiting the sick and ailing in Hospital. For some reason she wanted me as her Vice Chairman and this was duly confirmed. We spent many hours working together and I was able to gain so much from her vast experience in dealing with patients, friends and the working with the unions. She set me many hard tasks, notably all the meetings and tribunals with the unions and I shall always remember her for her kindness to me especially at the time of my motoring accident. She was a great character who sought no fame, and I am sure in my mind she must have been offered some honour from the Queen, but such was her nature that such an honour would not be to her liking or fit her image and I am confident she must have rejected (politely) any such offer. Many years after she retired I was standing at a bus stop in Birkenhead and as the Bus arrived she stepped off and proceeded to have a conversation with me, politely informing the driver not to move off until she had finished talking to me! A wonderful lady who asked for nothing but gave all.

The main thrust now was the completion of Arrowe Park Hospital, and a reduction in many minor outlets such as day centres, nursing homes, and other unsuitable completely outdated buildings. Clatterbridge Hospital was to be updated and St Catherine's Hospital in Birkenhead was to undergo renovation and change of use. From this it was apparent that the new hospital, when completed,was not going to be big enough to contemplate doing everything planned and so this proved to be. However came the day when all was in place and the date for the Royal Visit for the Official Opening was agreed.

The work of members of any Authority such as this can be a little difficult to understand, but in the main the members make their decisions on management ruling after having obtained the advice of the appropriate Chief Officers and weighed it in the balance. In recent years this appears to have changed and the professional officers seem to have gained more dictatorial powers, possibly with having to attend to continual changing dictates of the Department of Health with their many, (often impossible) targets. My duties as Vice Chairman were to attend all briefing meetings, to take charge of the management side in all personnel matters and union disputes and to chair the management and staff consultancy committee meetings to just name a few.

As time moved on my experience grew and grew and the financial side now became fully understandable In 1984 economies were still required and amongst other things a recent study showed that Hoylake Cottage Hospital had become uneconomical to operate and it was therefore agreed that it should be closed, and so it fell to me to announce this to the unions and await their obvious objection, but it had to be nevertheless A curious twist to this was that a local protest group was formed and although I attended as an observer for the Authority I became involved and was appointed to be the Vice Chairman of a new Trust set up to re-open the Hospital aided by support from David Hunt the local Member of Parliament. It may be coincidental but my fourth term of membership was due to end in the next few weeks, which it did, and I was always left wondering if the Hoylake event caused this or was it just that the time had come for a change of membership, which happens, and should happen, from time to time. As I was now leaving, I was able to look back and consider a most interesting sixteen years in which I had learned so much about the National Health Service and all the wonderful work it has achieved since it's inception. I am asked many times as to why the NHS is in continual need of more financing and my reply is always to add that as people are living longer, medical knowledge is advancing, and in addition, there is a continual advance in pharmaceutical research which must always result in continuing demands on the finances. But visiting the Hospital recently I was surprised that the entrance to all corridors had acquired a logo in the floor tiles which read "THIS IS A CLEAN HANDS AREA". My immediate reaction was to think "SO it should be!" and then to think that well, it can't be once anyone has entered that part of the building. In any case it ought to be clean without having to put in an expensive logo. Was it a needless waste of money?

As a final postscript on my service with NHS Hospitals my Chairman Mrs Roberts wrote a very kind letter to me in which she said:

"It will come as no surprise that you will not be re-appointed to the Health Authority. I know I write not just for myself personally, but for the Health Authority and indeed the Staff, who have appreciated your help and support during the past sixteen years. I especially have always been grateful to you for your support when you were the Vice Chairman and I am now very happy that you will be taking on the responsibility of the Hoylake Cottage Hospital Trust. The loss to the Health Authority is to the gain of this organisation."

CHAPTER NINETEEN

The Widening Scene

I think for my part one half of the World is Mad
and the other half not very sound.
- Tobias Smollett

In 1977 I brought to a conclusion my service with the Scouting Movement having given just over ten years as Group Scout Leader of the Hilbre Group of Scouts at Hoylake. In addition I had served as a District Scouter, and on the Wirral District Scout Council and also the rather onerous and tedious job as Badge Secretary for the District. During that time both John and Peter had been involved in the group, in which for a time John also served as a Scouter, coming home on Friday evenings from his University studies in Manchester. He was also involved in taking a number of Scouts to Switzerland together with the Meols Group and I have often wondered how he managed to deal with a trip that was not without many complications. There was a reciprocal visit by the Scouts from Switzerland and I think I have mentioned their amazement that there was such a thing as "Tides" when the sea disappeared! In all those years and many years afterwards I have been amazed that men from all walks of life have never denied their involvement in the movement, and always recalled the benefits they had gained however brief might have been their involvement. I have always maintained that if boys only join for one year they learn so much that affects their later life. In January 1977 I was delighted to be informed that I had been awarded "The Chief Scout's Commendation" for my services to the Scout Movement and I have always been pleased that the time in this service was well spent, and as an additional bonus the fact that my two sons were involved at the same period in time.

A few years later a very important letter, addressed to Jean (by protocol) proved to be an invitation to attend one of the Royal Garden Parties at Buckingham Palace. in May of that year. Whilst this was a surprise for although I had been given a hint before, I never really expected it to materialise. We arranged to go by car and stay with John and his family who were now living in Watford. Excitement with the three grandchildren was even greater than mine! We then went into London by train found our hotel and at about midday Jean and I put on our fancy clothes for the event. At the appropriate time we then travelled by underground (our golden coach!) and alighted at Green Park Station. We then walked across Green Park, in glorious sunshine to the Mall, round the Victoria Memorial and up to the Palace gates. We then waited outside the gates together with many others both famous and ordinary, like us, until we were let in. Entering the Palace we were escorted through a few rooms until we came through into the garden itself. We were now divided into many lines of groups of people and duly placed in our appointed spot to await the arrival of the Royal Party. Whilst waiting we were entertained by two military bands, one each side of the lawns and they played from their repertoire alternately. When the Royal Party arrived the Duke of Edinburgh had been allocated to our group and he passed thc line being introduced to some and not others. I was lucky and he stopped by me passed a few words of enquiry about myself. He then turned to the person next to me who was a high ranking fire officer and said to him, *"Who's minding the shop whilst you are here!"* After the presentations the royal party retired to a marquee for their afternoon tea and we peasants retired to ours at the other end of the lawns. The tea was very limited and quite unexciting, but the whole atmosphere was enthralling. About an hour later the Royal Party went inside and the garden party now being over we now drifted slowly to the exit, and thus back into the real world after a short visit to fairyland. It was an experience that I will always treasure and I felt very grateful to have been part of one of the ceremonies of this our country even if only a very minor part.

We then drifted into the West End, still all dressed up in our finery, and decided to have dinner in one of the many choices before us. Whilst having a meal, an American gentleman came to our table and seeing us dressed as we were asked us where we had been. He was most interested and so complimentary that I almost believed he thought we were very important and famous people, continually congratulating us on having had tea with the Queen!. He was most impressed and almost grateful for having heard our story of the afternoon which he was going to tell to his friends when he returned to America. The next day we returned to Watford and were obliged to go over each and every detail with Hannah, Louise and Amy. Little did they realise that they too, many years later, would enjoy this experience when their father was the recipient of a similar invitation. Unfortunately Hannah was the odd one out in that because as she was now married she was not classed as an "eligible daughter" as was the protocol.

In 1990 I received a letter from the Australian Institute of Pharmacy Management advising me that they had appointed me a Fellow of their organisation in recognition of the work I had conducted with them over a long period when I was the General Secretary of our own Institute. I was not really expecting that any contribution I had made would be other than treated as being in my line of day to day working with them. I received this with great pleasure and only regret that time overtook my being able to further their interests. Two years later I received a letter, as did Jean also, from the Royal Pharmaceutical Society congratulating both of us one reaching 50 years on the Register. Whilst this was very pleasing it did underline the fact that we were both now in our "Seventies" and underlined the long time that we had both been in the profession and reminded us of the various places and times we had been in practice. Whilst it was very pleasing to be recognised no one is particularly pleased to be reminded of the advancing years. Whilst my career had many variables over the years,I suppose the business and political side represented my professional career, in contrast Jean was a better practical and more medically inclined pharmacist. This was a very interesting division and outwardly it might appear at times that our objectives in life were quite divergent I now believe that on reflection it was mainly a different expression of the same objectives.

Whilst I am trying to keep dates of events in chronological order, I find that this has not proved to be too easy, and I apologise for any confusion caused.

In 1991 we were invited to attend a celebration given by the Corporation of London to mark the 150th Anniversary of the Royal Pharmaceutical Society. My invitation came by way of my membership of the Statutory Committee and of that body, I will refer to in a later chapter. Needless to say this was a splendid occasion attended by The Lord Mayor, the two Sheriffs with the escort for the Lord Mayor provided by the Company of Pikemen and Musketeers and many Aldermen and Commoners were in attendance. An exhibition of City Treasures was held in the Guildhall and this was followed by an elaborate buffet with music in the Great Hall provided by the Band of the Honourable Artillery Company. This was a splendid evening and was certainly enjoyed by both of us and it was reported at great length in the next days edition of the Daily Telegraph. This illustrated only too well the spin off advantages that occur by my giving of my time to national organisations. This was further followed in the next year when I received an invitation, again as a member of the Statutory Committee, to a reception to celebrate the 150th Anniversary to be held in the Society's Headquarters in Lambeth High Street London. On this occasion this was held in the presence of Her Majesty the Queen and His Royal Highness the Duke of Edinburgh. I was sent the details of where I would stand at the reception and a most memorable occasion followed, which I shall long remember and to which again I was very honoured to be invited.

Two events in 1994 come back to mind. Early in that year I received a letter to inform me I had been appointed to be an Honorary Auditor of the Pharmaceutical Society. This is a strange office, as there are six Honorary Auditors who meet only once a year so that the accountants can present the Balance Sheet and it to be approved before publication to the members. A quite unique appointment which I held for the next few years. The other event was when, in that year, I advised the National Pharmaceutical Association (our Union!) that I no longer wished to continue my membership. I had, after, all been a member since 1949 and had continued to be so for some ten years after I retired. The Secretary was a Tim Astill, who at one time had been a scholar at Kings School Chester (long after I left) and he wrote to me as follows:

'My colleagues of our Membership Department have passed me your letter of 10th October. I really find it impossible to believe you are approaching your seventy fifth Birthday, perhaps you would let me into your secret when we meet! In the meantime, everyone here at Mallinson House joins with me in sending you very best wishes for continued good health in your retirement. May I personally thank you for your friendship over the years and for all the support you have given to the NPA since 1949."

I tell this story chiefly because I was saddened and astonished to learn that Tim Astill had died suddenly a year after this letter. This was a great loss both for me personally and for our profession as a whole. He was sadly missed for he was a bundle of energy and drive.

An invitation to serve as Commodore to Hoylake sailing Club came in 1997. This was quite unexpected as the normal routes to Commodore are by serving as Rear and then Vice Commodore before elevation. In my case, due to a gap appearing in the 'chain' there was to be a vacancy. In my case I had not been able to take these Flag Officers positions in earlier years as my workload both with the business and other appointments prevented this happening.

However as I had been Honorary Treasurer for seven years and twenty seven years as a Director I suppose it was concluded that this was an opportunity to recognise my service to the Club. I was delighted to accept this opportunity and for the next two years apart from the club events I visited all the local kindred clubs for their Dinners and celebrations. Amongst all these visits I recall speaking at Wallasey Yacht Club Dinner when I told the them how I was in charge of a club that had a useless Committee but over four hundred experts sitting round the Bar! This went down so well that I concluded that I was not alone with this problem. During my term of office I was also to receive a letter from the Royal Mersey Yacht Club informing me I had been appointed a Life Member. The Commodore Tony Tetley wrote "It gives me great pleasure to advise you that at the General Committee Meeting held on 15th January 1996, it was unanimously agreed that you be offered Honorary Membership of the Royal Mersey Yacht Club in recognition of your services to the club. These services encompass two periods as Honorary Treasurer, a period as Honorary Auditor and some twenty five years a wise and committed member of the General Committee. All this in spite of your many professional, public service and extra mural commitments. It was felt that Honorary Membership should be offered to you at this particular time in your very active "Golden Years" when you are enjoying the honour of being Commodore of Hoylake Sailing Club."

The following year I received a letter from Hoylake Sailing Club Secretary who wrote, *"I write to confirm that on the fourteenth December 1999 the General Committee voted to offer you Life Membership of Hoylake Sailing Club"*. This concluded two notable and much appreciated events, and certainly brought great joy to me in my retiring years.

CHAPTER TWENTY

Hoyale Cottage Hospital

VENI VIDI VICI

- Julius Caesar

In a previous Chapter I spoke of the 1983 closure of the NHS Hoylake Cottage Hospital which came about by Wirral Health Authority being obliged to make economies at that time. This caused great consternation and anger amongst the people living in Meols, Hoylake and West Kirby resulting in the calling of a protest meeting. This was attended by Wirral Health Authority representatives and I was appointed to serve on a joint meeting of both parties to consider this impasse. Following this meeting a Local Steering Committee was set up and I attended as Vice Chairman of Wirral Health Authority. The result was a firm determination to re-open the Hospital as a Trust and a promise from our MP David Hunt resulted in some monies being found from one of the many Government "secret" funds. I now found myself elected as Vice Chairman and the Trustees appointed were, a retired Education Guidance Officer, Chairman of the League of friends, a Medical Practitioner and myself, a Pharmacist. David Hunt was appointed as our President The Trustees then formed the company Hoylake Cottage Hospital Trust Ltd and George Eustance was appointed Chairman and myself Vice Chairman. With monies from the Government and the Regional Health Authority support and others we were now able to re-open the hospital on a five year lease granted by the NHS. This was to be the first time throughout the whole of England that an NHS hospital had been reopened as a private venture.

In the midsummer of 1984 the hospital came back to life. There were many difficulties to be overcome and the first was to tidy up the mess left after the (rather hasty?) departure on the closure. Sadly the place was full of rubbish, and, worse still one of the rooms was full of scattered patient records all of which had been left behind. We had great difficulty in disposing of these but eventually they were taken away. The next stage was to fit out the wards and kitchens, engage staff, and indoctrinate them in the rudiments of change over from NHS employment, and costings. The main objectives were to develop a community based establishment principally caring for the elderly with special attention to be devoted to the provision of respite care to give relief to those looking after infirm relatives at home. In addition a Day Centre for the elderly was to be provided which enabled them to have a day away from home and to provide additional other services such as hairdressing, shampooing and chiropody.. In addition entertainment was to be provided after the lunch time in the afternoon. The day centre was manned by teams drawn from over two hundred volunteers and proved a great help and success. As time went on we were also to embrace facilities for Alzheimer's patients with expert professional help to cover this. Volunteers were also used as bedmakers, typists, gardeners, ambulance drivers, fund raisers and many other associated duties. The response by local citizens was remarkable, and I am sure it was never envisaged that so many would offer their services. The league of friends were now able to man the reception desk in the entrance hall which again meant that the employed staff were able to attend to their duties without interruption.

After the first few months it became very apparent that George Eustance the Chairman was far from well and I was asked to take over the Chairmanship and the responsibility of running the hospital. George was immediately made Vice President which was richly deserved in view of the energies he had put in to bring about this whole project. His forte was publicity, and this had been used to such good effect. For the next three years I worked virtually full time at the hospital having to deal with the many early teething troubles and the diminishing lack of funding, although many varied methods were used in local fund raising and in addition the work and results in the Cottage Hospital Shop, which we had now opened were of enormous assistance At the end of the first year it became apparent that despite the good intentions and energies of the first appointed committee there was not enough professional business experience to provide the weight required. This was no reflection on these committee members but they had been drawn from those who believed in the project as a desirable need for the elderly but were unfortunately without the requirements for being effective on the financial and practical side. I was then able to persuade two very important and successful local business men to join the committee and this added great strength and experience to our workings.

My main objective now was to see that the hospital remained open, despite the gloomy predictions of many friends and even one or two local organisations.

Indeed the outlook did look bleak but I had set a target of three years to establish a state of affairs that would enable us to see further into the future. To increase further our income a Fund Raising Officer was appointed and an approach was made to local solicitors so that they could advise clients, when making their will, that money given by them would be used to good effect for the benefit of the community. This approach proved quite useful as we now became in receipt of a number of legacies from time to time. By now the former Nurses Wing had been converted into a number of flats by the efforts of a separate set of volunteers and these proved to be a great success and were in great demand. This did not form a part of the hospital services but were a set of fee paying rooms with a housekeeper to manage the flats and provide mid day meals. This now brought a further well needed income. President David Hunt advised us that he had used his position to persuade the Queen Mother to give a donation and in addition arrangements were being made for a visit to the Hospital by HRH The Prince of Wales. The visit was arranged for 22nd May 1987 and as the day approached there was feverish activity by the security services and the Lord Lieutenant's Office. The day before the visit we received a message that the royal visitor would not be coming. and although I was the recipient of a letter from his Private Secretary Sir John Riddell the disappointment was quite depressing to the many volunteers, and indeed the preparations had proved to be a totally unnecessary waste of our meagre funds. I understood the reason was a clash of dates that had been made whilst the Prince as abroad. This was really no solace!

Towards the end of 1987 it became very apparent that the hospital was operating at a loss and with a desire not to lose all that had been gained over the last three years and not to have wasted all the efforts made by so many volunteers, the best advice available was to go into administration. This being a method by which a firm of accountants would operate the company and attempt to return the Finances into a more stable condition. Despite my personal disappointment I felt that if this could see us through then this was the best and only way to proceed. On the 2nd of October the court granted this administration application and Mr Frank Taylor of Messrs Arthur Young the Liverpool Accountants was appointed Administrator. The next months were indeed full of frustration for me for as Chairman as I was still actively involved, and my patience at times was sore tried. In July 1988 after sterling work by Frank Taylor and his associates the time had now arrived for the handover back to the company and at this point it was agreed that a new Chairman be appointed. This was really not difficult for me to accept because the past three years had been very onerous and it now looked that my determination to get the hospital through it's growing pains and on to a stable basis had been achieved. At the time I felt that I had failed and this lived with me for a long time afterwards, until common sense persuaded me I was being too harsh on myself. My departure from the committee was very short lived for I was back as an appointed committee member some two years later!

The newly appointed Chairman was a William Zuydam, who lived in Caldy was a retired senior employee of the Lever Brothers Organisation. He had held many senior appointments and came to us with a wealth of experience behind him. Before taking over he spent many meetings and many hours with me in seeking to know all about the reopening and the past three years. Whilst he pursued this with me he was very through and strong minded so much so that I felt at times I was under interrogation. He hastened to tell me this was not so and I soon learned that this was the way he conducted business and I also learned a lot from him as well! He immediately appointed a General Manager, a former employee of the Ford Company, and later a new and very experienced part time Matron and in addition gathered a new team around him with one or two of us "left overs" being incorporated. There was a continuing programme of building improvements and as a result a more improved layout of the space became available. It now became apparent also that the age of the building was causing problems as the continuing new regulations were not able to be fully integrated, this resulting in the hospital not obtaining the full grants from Social Services for the patients placed in the Cottage Hospital by them. In addition further reports showed that the building itself was proving to be a hazard in that it did not comply with the building regulations, chiefly because bits had been added on from time to time over the last hundred years. The Chairman's main policy was that of continual improvements in the provision for the patients and improved staffing but most of all he fought for funds. His policy was that the hospital should amass a strong financial reserve, which, in addition, would give a good return as an investment. This was at a time when interest on funds was at a high level. After many years of service and progress he felt that the time had come to hand over the Chairmanship as he probably felt that he had given all he could and perhaps he felt that despite all his energies the hospital was ready for a further change of management and, indeed, he could not continue giving his time and energies ad infinitum. He did a superb piece of service and was the right man at the right time. I fully enjoyed working with him over the many years. and we became great friends.

The next Chairman of the Trust was Michael Taylor who throughout a varied business career had at one time been connected with a pharmaceutical manufacturing company in Northern Ireland. I never found out any more about his experience and he never told me! Naturally he brought many new ideas and he also built up a new team of directors as and when change was necessary. In contrast to his predecessor his view for the future was modernising the hospital and a complete new form of management. His vision was for a complete replacement of the present buildings this being enforced by the need to have more beds available in order to be financially sound. This vision of his was going to need large sums of money and despite his management ideas being different to his predecessor he was nevertheless grateful for William Zydam's policy of building a large fund for future use. Before this could take place and as new expertise came to join the team many management studies were made and in addition from time to time full day seminars were held. The strategy now evolving was to be the provision of a completely new hospital with sixty beds and complete new service facilities.

The commencement of this project was to engage a firm of architects to draw up a plan for discussion. As this proceeded the public were to be made aware of the project. This produced many angry reactions which could have been anticipated. In the first place we were eventually to lose the old Hospital which did not endear the board to the public who wanted the future to be like the present, and in addition the design and height of the new building was felt to be an outrage to the nearby community. After many months and after many alterations the plans were approved. The financing was to be a large programme and the expertise on the board became of invaluable with their help and experience gained in their various professions. Eventually the day came to commence the building of the new hospital, but not before many many plans had to be made and implemented so that the existing hospital and patients would not be disrupted. Great credit is due to the matron and her staff for their advice and help in this difficult time. A further disruption in that the Day Centre could not now operate on the premises and was now to be removed to an external site for the time being. This was a very difficult decision but it had to be made and whilst the return is not immediate the future plans do provide for this.

Early in 2009 the Hospital was completed, start was made in moving patients and an Official Opening was held in February. The well designed building now blends perfectly with the local buildings and is an obvious success and a great tribute to all who made it possible. There is still need of more donations but the remainder of the cost has been borne on an agreed loan and the forward planning shows that there are sound reasons that the hospital will be solvent and able to meet its commitments. This is largely due to the endless meetings held in seeking ways to bring this about. The district, after twenty five years of work and practical contribution by local people, together with considerable local support, has a new sixty bed modern hospital to continue the story of over 100 years of service to this community. That the whole project over the last quarter century is a success there is no doubt and shows what can be done if the will is there to do so, and thanks must be given for the willing dedication of so many friends of the new "Cottage".

CHAPTER TWENTYONE

Wirral Postgraduate Medical Centre

DISPLACEMENT ACTIVITY
Frantic activity with Non Essentials
When faced with really difficult problems

Perhaps this cryptic opening will be best understood by the General Manager of the Centre!

When I first became a member of Wirral Area Health Authority I was seconded as the person to represent the Health Authority on the hitherto new and unknown Postgraduate Medical Centre which was situated in the grounds of Clatterbridge Hospital. It appears that a number of consultants, general practitioners and dentists had seized on the idea to promote and encourage postgraduate training together with a provision for socialising, and thus encouraged by the Chief Officer at Clatterbridge Hospital proceeded to obtain a lease for a section of land within the Hospital grounds, from the then Secretary of State for Social Services. The Centre was to be entirely independent of any other control and efforts were then made to find donations to further this project, and the response from a number of dignitaries and local companies, together with a £20,000 loan from the hospital enabled the project to proceed. A trust was then set up and charity status acquired and in 1973 for this purpose and then the building of the Centre took place. The modern designed building contained a library, an exhibition foyer together with administration offices on the ground floor, and the accommodation on the first floor was a large lecture theatre, a dining area and number of smaller rooms. The Centre was to be administered by a Centre Manager, and in addition some part time administration staff and library staff, their salaries coming from the Regional Health Authority and later the Mersey Deanery. Membership was to be for doctors and dentists only, and whilst other Health Service professions at that time felt they too should be able to partake of its facilities as members, this was not to be. The new Trust appointed four Trustees and an Executive Committee representing the professions involved, and in 1974 a representative from Liverpool Regional Heath Authority and myself representing Wirral Area Health Authority were also included.

In 1974 the new Wirral Health Authority came into being and with it a whole new and broader approach to medical provision. On 17th June I received a letter from the Secretary of the Centre inviting me to my first meeting of the Executive Committee he having been advised of my secondment. Whilst the arrangements for running the centre had been implemented I was at first quite confused as to who did what, for although the Executive Committee met frequently the Trustees met no more than twice a year and although this appeared to work I had a worrying feeling that something was not quite right about this arrangement, and some twenty five years later this thought was vindicated when our legal adviser informed me that the Trustees were the only managers of the Trust and it's day by day workings.

But more of that later. At that time the Centre had appointed volunteer medical and dental tutors and for many years these posts were held by a number of successive volunteers This worked well and many educational courses and other allied events were arranged. Many years later the NHS gave a more positive indication that continuing medical and dental training was overdue and from then tutors in all departments of medicine and dentistry were appointed by the Deanery and the Health Authority. This rather left this new Centre as a provider of facilities for Education rather than being ,as hitherto,the actual educational providers. In the early years the Executive Committee and it's Social Committee were also engaged in providing social events, dinners, dining facilities and lettings for weddings and private parties. Over the years the demand for this diminished, due largely to changing times as there had developed a resistance to coming back in the evening to the "workplace". For the first five years we held an Annual Dinner but the final one that was held proved to be quite a disaster as the caterer ran out of food half way through the serving and half those present had to wait over an hour for their food! The use of this sort of facility for personal events had not proved popular and in recent years useage has been minimal The early meetings of the Social Committee were usually held at the residence of one of its members and these seemed to prove more entertaining and popular than the fare they were supposed to be arranging!

After the first four years the very popular Hon. Treasurer died and at the meeting following this I found myself appointed to take his place much to my surprise this being a salutary example of what happens when you send apologies for absence from a meeting (as I did on this occasion)! I suppose I was really quite flattered and it did appear to be something useful that I could do. About this time a new General Manager had been appointed and so both of us were starting together on new ground and it was the formation of a partnership which is still in place all these years later. My first task was to set about putting the financial paperwork in order as no proper accounts appeared to have been carried out for the previous six years and I still do not understand how the Charities Commission accepted this, but perhaps they were not so strict as they are now. The work of the Executive had been well documented and carried out but the Trustees section dealing with Investments and Subscriptions had just been placed in a filing cabinet to await attention at some time in the future. After a few months this had all been attended to and the auditors (who had given their services at no cost,) eventually brought things up to date.

The Trust had been fortunate in that they had acquired the gratuitous services of both solicitors and accountants for the formation and for a few years afterwards. Together with the General Manager, Barbara Rice, we arranged a system that I should keep all the books and payments for the day to day work and she would service a separate account for the interest on Treasury Investments and the subscriptions and tax claims on Covenants. At the end of the year I was to bring all this together and prepare all details for the accountants. I choose to mention this now for no one seems to know how we run the accounts as long as we produce the results. What happens if I decide not to continue is in the lap of the gods for there is no provision for financial expertise, so this may be a question of waiting until it happens!

After twelve years my appointment to the Health Authority came to an end and this also meant that I would not be able to continue as a member of the Postgraduate Centre. It would appear that this was not to the liking of the trust and they overcame their difficulty by appointing me an Honorary Member which was very flattering and whilst it had solved a problem I felt that my work and dedication had been noted and approved, and as in 2009 I am still there I can honestly feel that the honour has now been more than justified. Having now arranged a procedure for the finances I started to visit each week to deal with any work on hand and to discuss with Barbara any problems and planning matters and in this way she was able to bounce off various problems to me and we could throw them about and most often see a way through the matter in hand. The usage of the centre continued to grow and although the financing was difficult we managed to come through each year and just about achieve a small surplus. It always has disturbed be greatly that the income for most of the courses came from the drug manufacturers which whilst appearing acceptable within the "Health Service," these firms should not be subsidising costs that should truly belong to the National Health Service. If it wants its professionals to have further training, which it should, then it should be prepared to fund the costs. Many events and changes have taken place over the last thirty years and whilst I mention some I cannot guarantee that the chronological order is correct for this is a recall of memory without any notes to guide me. One of the continuing problems has always been the provision of car parking any many attempts at solving this have come and gone. But I do recall that we nearly got it right when an arrangement (I will not call it an agreement) was made with the Oncology Centre to move their library into our existing library and in return we would gain access at certain times to the car park. This meant the enlargement of the library, with the loss of the foyer and a complete refurbishing, but alas the car park problem has stayed with us. Over the years we have replaced and added to the equipment, completely renewed the seating in the lecture theatre and yet all this has had to be met from our funds despite the fact that the use of all this is mainly by the Hospital Trust, and I have always thought that not enough attention was paid to this at the start, when more positive understanding of the needs could have been arranged though I would agree that conditions were much different before 1974. This is a personal view and does not seem to cause the same worry to some others, the confusion of who does what, or pays for what continues to this day.

In 1997 the rapid advance in the use of computers within the medical and dental services produced the initiation by the Dental Dean and others of an IT Vocational Training Unit which was funded by the Deanery and was integrated in the larger lecture room on the first floor embracing all the latest technology and teaching expertise. This flourished for many years but the need eventually diminished as more and more dentists became computer literate and modern programming filled their needs more appropriately. There were now discussions taking place to move this unit to the ground floor and combine it with the library facilities, but nothing has been finalised at this time. Some ten years ago it was becoming apparent that the Trust Deed had now become out- dated chiefly by the passage of time, and it was agreed to start discussions to amend this and to bring the rules up to date. Many discussions were held, and many ideas came and went and finally it was decided that the General Manager and myself should arrange a meeting to discuss this with the Trust' Solicitor. At this point the four trustees came to the decision that the time had come to terminate their period of office, which they had held for many many years and would await the outcome of any revision of the Trust before moving to a well deserved retirement. The outcome of this consultation was the production of a Declaration of Trust, which superseded the original one, allowed for the retirement of the four trustees and the appointment of new trustees, three of whom were listed in the new deed and these could be added to as felt appropriate the number eventually arriving at six trustees. This brought the working of the Trust Deed and all its clauses up to date and in particular clearly stated that the total management of the trust was to be by the trustees only, though if necessary sub committees could be appointed for particular problems.

The present state of affairs has now produced some confusion partly because the original terms of funding and staffing have now come into question and the increasing influence of the hospital management in challenging some of the costings and salary sources and as to what charges the Postgraduate Centre can made for those parts of the building no longer under the Postgraduate Centre Management. This is a problem that must now be solved and a clearer and more positive relationship must be brought about. It should however be noted that at the commencement of this project in 1973 the conditions were so different and this coupled with the problem that some of the trustees are employed by the Hospital Trust which can make decisions by them very difficult at times. I am confident that over the next year or two a resolution will be found, but only after many legal and other problems have been solved. For my part I would add that I always tried to give advice where I could and I am sure that when I leave I will feel that I have helped in no small way to further the objects and ambitions of those who brought the Wirral Postgraduate Medical centre into being and whose foresight at that time was well in advance of the thinking and the needs of that time.

CHAPTER TWENTYTWO

The Statutory Commitee of the Royal Pharmaceutical Society

Oh, what a tangled web we weave
When first we practise to deceive
- Sir Walter Scott

During my long career as a pharmacist, on receiving the Pharmaceutical Journal each week I had little or no interest in the page given over to the workings of something called the Statutory Committee as it appeared to be something that was presided over by a Judge appointed by the Privy Council. Perhaps little interest is not quite the word for in reality I found its workings difficult to absorb and understand. .But I knew it was important.

By 1989 I felt that the end had been reached in my voluntary appointments,with the exception of a now diminished role with the Cottage Hospital so it was a great surprise to receive a phone call from the Secretary of the Pharmaceutical Society. At the time I was occupied with an afternoon locum at my former pharmacy and I was also surprised therefore that I had been assumed to be there. The call by John Ferguson {who was then the Secretary) was to the effect that The President and Vice President of the Pharmaceutical Society wished to put my name forward for nomination to fill a vacancy as a member of the Statutory Committee and were about to go into the Council Meeting to make this proposal if I was willing to serve. Needless to say I was delighted. On the 8th June 1989 I received a letter from the society to the effect that I had been appointed to the Statutory Committee and requesting me to attend the first meting in July. I was also requested to send my C.V. and photograph to circulate to the other members. I was the 31st Member to be so appointed since the commencement of the committee under the 1932 Pharmacy Act. The Committee consisted of a Chairman who must me a senior QC or a retired Judge and five appointed members (one of whom must be from Scotland) appointed as mentioned and confirmed by the Privy Council. Then I received a welcoming letter from the then Chairman Edward Sutcliffe QC and also from the one lady member Barbara Young a very notable hospital pharmacist who also served as a member of the General Medical Council

On arrival for the first Meeting I was introduced to the other four members who all seemed to be so well known in pharmacy circles, so I was more than surprised that they seemed overawed by my CV! The routine was soon learned and I discovered I would be attending monthly for four days at a time, and so I made arrangements with the Naval Club for a booking on a regular monthly basis. This was a very convenient arrangement as I had been a member of the Naval Club in London since its formation during the War. The hearings were more or less like the Magistrates Courts with perhaps more a leaning to the longer committal cases. It was very formal and during the four days a hearing of three or four cases might be heard, with perhaps, in some cases postponements if time ran out. The arrangements were for a specific number of cases to be heard each time but as the length of each case was variable, postponements were inevitable. The hearings were are held in public and as reporters are present so there is to be no escape for those in trouble. It is constantly said that these are kangaroo courts but that was far from the truth. Politicians seem to imagine that a "lay" representation was necessary in the "public interest" and though this is indefensible many years later they would have there way in a total re-organisation which I shall refer to later. From time to time the membership changes as the term of office of each member expires and whilst all newcomers were of great interest there are two I would wish to mention. The first was the appointment of a new Chairman which took place during my second year and Gary Flather, a prominent QC, became the new incumbent. Unfortunately many years earlier he had been stricken down with a paralysing illness which had affected his career and his very energetic athletic and public life. There is no doubt halted his progress in legal circles. Nevertheless he led a very active legal life despite the difficulty of of being wheelchair bound. Gary became a very personal friend as well and on my retirement much later his kind remarks about me left me in no doubt that I had been an effective member of the committee even if it did embarrass me a little! The second Member I would like to mention was Bill Rucker who came from Plymouth. Talking to him one day I discovered that he went for a time to Kings School at Chester, but only at the Junior school. Later his family must have moved elsewhere but I did discover that like myself he was a Justice of the Peace and in addition a Fellow of the Royal Pharmaceutical Society, which considering there we only five members in the Statutory Committee was quite an unusual co-incidence.

Experience of this regulatory arm of the Society has convinced me that members should try and visit it when it is in session and I am sure they would appreciate the true nature of how it defends and protects their profession. The two main objects of this committee which was set up in 1932 are the protection of the public at large and the protection of the honourable profession as a body. This all sounds a little pompous at first but if I elaborate on some of the facets of this protection then it becomes a little clearer. Firstly it not a "Off with his head" organisation but rather tends to be an understanding and human body dealing with the many pitfalls that pharmacists (and others) can fall in to in their daily life. Firstly it appears that real crime represents only about fifteen percent of the cases and also that over fifty percent of cases (as I write) can be associated with the actions of Asian pharmacists and this being largely because of their inability to understand they are operating under United Kingdom laws and customs, and in turn them finding this difficult to come to terms with. This I find is a great pity for it causes many misjudgements and opinions to be become confused. I am certain that within the next generation this problem may well have resolved itself. The Statutory Committee hears complaints that the Ethics Committee have decided are so serious as to merit further investigation. These complaints can come from a report from a member of the public, by way of court cases and also those brought by the Inspectors of the Society, who visit pharmacies on a regular basis and are thereby well able to advise pharmacists of possible errors or, if necessary, deem them serious enough to report to the Ethics Committee. It might be asked why do we need to embrace Ethics at all. Ethics in the Pharmaceutical profession deals with its members who fall by the wayside, this however, is not an act solely associated with this particular profession, and chiefly because working in the profession brings them constantly in contact with the general public they must therefore be seen to be trusted beyond reproach in all our dealings with them.

The misconducts that the committee may have to deal with are varied and can be for theft, deception, unlawful possession of drugs, drink Offences, motoring offences, fraud, sex offences, illegal trading, dirty premises to name a few. Decisions are made on the degree of severity and any mitigating circumstances. All offences must me deemed serious enough to require a removal from the register but if there are mitigating circumstances this can be reduced to an admonishment or a recorded reprimand. Mitigation can take many forms, for example, ill health, financial troubles, domestic upsets, business pressure, exploitation and fear just to name a few. But this is not an easy way out of avoiding being "struck off," and in all cases the pharmacist concerned has three months to put in an appeal to the High Court or a Judicial Review. I have mentioned earlier that the actions do not amount to intimidation but the details given above do give food for thought that there must be this form of regulation as members behaviour must always meet with approval by the public if it is seen to conduct its affairs fairly and openly.

There are of course many cases in which action should be immediate, and sometimes it is quite wrong that the pharmacist should continue to practice just because the regulations allow him three months to appeal. Sometimes this dilemma is overcome by mutual agreement which can at times remove immediate danger to the public. I have refrained from bringing in specific cases, but on reflection perhaps one or two simpler cases could be mentioned. One of these was that of when a pharmacist engaged a holiday locum for his two weeks holiday and left him a few signed cheques, just in case he needed to make an urgent payment. The Locum immediately made out a cheque for £20,000 opened a Post Office account and later on in the week drew out all the money! The pharmacy owner did not become aware of this until he received his next bank statement. Another case concerned a prescription for a 500 gram roll of cotton wool. The chemist claimed that the prescription was for 500 times 500 gram rolls, and duly claimed payment for this amount, which he had not supplied, and as a result quite rightly received a prison sentence and the Judge in the case on sentencing him to one years imprisonment, remarked that it would need a furniture removal van to collect such a quantity! On appearing one year later,on release from prison, he was quite rightly removed from the Register. This once again revived the conflict about double jeopardy where he appeared to have received two punishments, but that is open to debate and the subject of a long standing legal battle that goes on and on. These are two examples of simpler cases but others could present difficult problems and take many days to complete. There was however no mileage for those who transgress and then try to claim ignorance by saying they didn't know the law, for by the very fact that they are registered members they would have been taught and should know what is required before final qualification as a pharmaceutical chemist. In fact such a plea was an insult to all present and was not tolerated. Over the next five years I travelled to London once a month, arriving Monday evening and departing Friday morning. It was only after I had ceased to being a member of this committee that I realised just how much of my time this was occupying each month. Nevertheless I will always be satisfied that I was chosen to judge my peers and the experience gained in so many ways added to the overall picture of all the various facets of life throughout the years, and I am most honoured and grateful that this opportunity came my way The end of my appointment came very abruptly. It had been fully anticipated that I would be reappointed for a further five years, but unknown to me the Pharmaceutical Society had been under pressure from the Equal Opportunities Board to appoint an Asian representative to the Statutory Committee and this happened to coincide with the conclusion of my five year appointment. Much to the surprise of all, and in particular the Chairman, as I arrived for what was to be my last attendance I was informed I would not be reappointed. At first I was sure I must have done something wrong, but after explanation the whole matter was resolved and the Chairman in a very detailed statement, which flattered me, bade me farewell from which I quote:

"Speaking personally, and I think I speak for the rest of the Committee, I have always been reassured if Geoffrey is reassured because he is not someone you can bowl many balls fast without him noticing, and if he feels happy about something then I feel enormously reassured."

But I know that he was very upset as to how this whole matter had been conducted without even having the courtesy of being told what was taking place.

On reflection I had no regrets for by this time I had reached the age of 83 years and now felt that a further term would have proved very hard and tiring. The companionship of those years has remained and I now meet with my former members each year just before Christmas. As I write, great changes are taking place, the Pharmaceutical Society is about to lose the regulatory powers to a new body called the General Pharmaceutical Council, which is yet another government creation to see that lay people are visibly represented on this and similar organisations. The Statutory Committee of a Chairman and five Members meeting once a month is now replaced by Disciplinary Committee consisting of a group of so forty appointees who will have only four pharmacists on it, and ten of these appointees now meet every day of the week to hear cases. I can hardly believe that the irrational behaviours of some pharmacists has increased just because of this change!!

CHAPTER TWENTYTHREE

Millennium

Retirement is the time of life when you can stop lying about your age and start lying about the house

Throughout my whole life I had never envisaged living in the year 2000 and I was therefore very surprised to find myself in my eightieth year standing at the dawn of a new century. At the time it really was a strange sensation for as a child it was just something in the stars. Once the realisation had dawned life did not seem to have changed at all and things seemed to be carrying on just as before.

For some time we had been thinking of reducing the size of the garden and selling off the front part for the planning and building of a house. We had been approached many times over the years by various developers who in the end took no action as it always appeared that it would not be possible to fit in a house in the width available, even supposing plans would be approved by the Council I then approached an architect friend and asked him what he could do for us. He went away and a few weeks later came back with details for a three bedroom house which would fit in the plot and would be identical both to the adjoining main house and our cottage. To the surprise of many people, or maybe it was influence, the Plans were finally accepted after great protest from next door neighbours on both sides and other house owners around. The ground and plans were then put up for tender and there were about four offers, including one from one of our next door neighbours!

Finally one of the offers was accepted and although it did not quite come up to the price estimated it was, however, almost ten times what we had paid for house and all the land some thirty three years before. After a two month delay building commenced and our view of the sea disappeared and whilst we had some regrets we had been left with a landscaped smaller garden which was more manageable and suited to us, and as a bonus we were no longer as troubled by high winds and storms. The new house was sold for £250,000 and two years later was sold again for some £400,000 thus keeping apace with the outrageous rise in house prices early in the early years of the millennium. I just add this in passing and make no comment on how much Seaways Cottage might possibly sell for now even much more saleable with its new enclosed landscaped garden. But then, there's really no need to know.

In 2000 I joined the Grange Probus Club, a Luncheon Dining Club for retired businessmen. Formerly there had been three local Probus Clubs (should it be Probi?) the first two having been brought into being by me when I was extension officer in Hoylake Rotary Club, so it seemed strange that I should end up in the one I had not created. I had been hoping for many years previously to join the Hoylake one but was always told there were no vacancies! During my first three years as a new member I was called upon to give a talk, which I did, and gave them a potted version of my MTB experiences. They seemed to like this talk so much that a year later they asked me to speak again. I wondered what on earth I could give that was of interest to them and eventually gave a talk on my work with the Statutory Committee of the Royal Pharmaceutical Society. This went down as well or if not even better than the first one! In 2005 I was elected Chairman of the Club and I thoroughly enjoyed my year of office. This included a coach holiday in Edinburgh and the Kingdom of Fife and though I am a very bad coach traveller I was able to enjoy the five day holiday. I am now back as an ordinary member, enjoy my lunch each month and most times stay fully awake for the talk afterwards.

In 1988 we had purchased a Mid February two week holiday villa in Playa Blanca in Lanzarote on an estate owned then by Wimpeys. At the time of purchase it was just an uncompleted shell and we were a little concerned on our first visit the next year to see if all was well. The villa proved to be all they had promised and we had a small front garden full of flowers to enjoy our relaxation. This holiday was looked forward to each February and each year we watched the expansion of Playa Blanca from a small fishing village into a thriving holiday resort. Over the years we made many friends and grew to love the place as though it was our home. Gerald Armstrong my brother in law spent a number of visits with us and our friends John and Margaret Spence also purchased a villa and in time so did both their sons. By 2002 we were considering selling the villa particularly because Jean's health was deteriorating and travelling was becoming a little difficult for her. Towards the end of the year the deal was completed and it was with with some regret this annual holiday had come to an end. However there was a brief reprieve before the final departure because in 2003 we joined with the Spence's to share their villa for yet another year, but as Jean had been quite unable to cope with the travelling it was now realised that there could be no further visits.

Early in May it became apparent that Jean was far from well, but it was in keeping with her strong character that she kept her privacy intact until during the day on 12th May she told me that she had fallen over in the bedroom and on coming down to tell me this she collapsed on the floor in the lounge. I found it impossible to lift her and the lady from next door came and helped me get her into her armchair. Whether it was great respect for her privacy or just her nature, I still wonder as to why at this time I took no action. However at 9pm it was very apparent that something was wrong and when I tentatively suggested a 999 call she readily agreed, much to my surprise. She was taken to Arrowe Park and she immediately sent me away to buy her a newspaper! At nine o'clock in the evening! When I returned she had been put into a bed and on my arrival she held out a £10 Note and told me to go home and have a "Sneck Lifter" on the way home. Translated from the Cumbria Dialect this meant buy yourself a drink. Those were to be her very last words spoken to me, for in the days that followed she remained in a coma and eventually in the middle of the night on 16th May she passed away. I had been called to the hospital and Peter and Hannah were with me. After the funeral I continued to live at Seaways Cottage and although I felt I was managing, many comments were passed that I was going down and not looking after myself. I received great support and kindness from many friends but perhaps in particular from Carole Jackson who apart from kindness made sure I went out at least one evening a month to wine and dine with her. This was a friendship formed many years ago serving on the Finance Committee of the Lifeboat and this strong and understanding friendship still continues to this day.

The last thing anyone should do is to predict what the future might hold, and so it proved in my case. Being now some 84 years of age I believed that I would be spending the remaining years of my life in Seaways Cottage backed up by paid helpers until such time as I might have to be looked after elsewhere. At that time my evening refuge was turning out to be Hoylake Sailing Club where I could enjoy the evening with my many friends. At that time also one of the ladies behind the bar was someone who was working at the Club in the evening in addition to her daytime occupation. I say, with diffidence, she was much more senior in years than the other staff and was a well liked personality by the members.

To my surprise, and maybe hers, we developed an interest in each other which resulted in my asking her out to have a meal with me one evening. This was at first just a one off, but it grew into a stronger friendship and after many long hours of heart searching by her she agreed to come and share her life with me. No sooner had this happened than she was taken ill with gallstones and rushed off to hospital, returning about week later when she was recovering. About this time I had arranged to go on a Cruise with a family friend Dick Ellison and during the second week I was awoken by a phone call from Hoylake asking me where the "Stop Cock" was at Seaways Cottage. The reasons don't matter but surely this could only be the development of something greater and on my return from the Cruise I proposed to Colleen and she agreed to be my wife. I am sure Colleen does not mind me pointing out that she was thirty years younger than me, for the secret was bound to come out later. In passing, to be about to marry someone who was a year younger than my eldest son was quite an unusual experience.

On 20th August 2004 we were married at the Registry Office at Birkenhead Town Hall in the presence of my family and a few friends. The arrangements for the day were in the capable hands of the best man John Percival and his wife Maureen. Both of them did everything to make the day a success even to the provision of a Rolls Royce for our return journey home. The luncheon was held at the Kings Gap Hotel and best man's arrangements for us were superb. Here I might say that John was almost unknown to me until I became Commodore in 1997 when he was the Club Secretary. We rapidly became friends and shared the tasks of those few years which had the added bonus of a bonding respect for each other and he often referred to me as his second father. I will never know the first reactions of John and Peter and the various members of the family and the conversations that might have followed, but I have always been pleased that there has been an acceptance of the marriage, though for some it took a little time. Since then Colleen has become one of the family and keeps well in contact with the grandchildren and now great grandchildren.

Since the Wedding we have travelled to many places firstly to Malta and later to Edmonton in Canada for the wedding of Colleen's only daughter Gillian. The actual wedding took place in the Rockies and was an open air affair at a kind of youth hostel. Happily the arrangements for us consisted of a lovely log cabin set in beautiful surroundings. A year later we visited Gillian again who was now living in Halifax Nova Scotia. This was a most interesting and historical place and we found plenty to occupy our time. Since then we have visited Lanzarote twice and on the first occasion motored to Playa Blanca to visit the Las Brisas Compound once again and even found some of my former friends who were on holiday there. I was also very pleased that I was able to take Colleen to a lunch at the Headquarters of the Royal Pharmaceutical Society in London. This was an annual occasion when the members and former members of the Statutory Committee meet for a renewal of friendships and a talk about old times and experiences shared.

A very sad event in my life occurred in the summer of 2007 when I received the news that my old Naval friend Bert Fry had died after a long illness. He was Bert Fry to me but to most of his friends he was Teddy Fry, I think he felt it more appropriate name for a Naval Officer. We met for the first time at HMS King Alfred in Brighton when we were striving for a Commission. We both made it and he became Midshipman Fry (because he was only eighteen years old,) and I became Sub/Lieut Knowles. We then moved to Greenwich College in London (allegedly to learn how to hold a knife and fork!). That is not strictly true but many years passed before I discovered out why we went to this illustrious place and dined in the Great Hall with the King (present only on Thursdays), the reason being that as potential Coastal Forces Officers we would not get the early experience of being junior officers by going to the routine of "Big Ships". We had both been selected to go the HMS St. Christopher at Fort William in Scotland for training in motor torpedo boats. On completion we were appointed to different Boats in different flotillas and only met from time to time during the next few years. We had become great friends and on demobilisation we met from time to time. He had elected to follow me and become a pharmacist and ultimately had his own business in Malvern. For a short time we operated a company franchising generic tablets and other pharmaceutical necessities and trading with many other Chemists. Part of the operation of this business required us to meet at regular intervals to exchange stock, or for me to obtain further supplies. To effect this we each journeyed to a pub car park midway between Malvern and Hoylake and proceeded to pass stock and other goods from one car to the other. Whilst this never seemed to arouse much interest, I am quite sure that today we could well have been arrested and accused of "drug smuggling". (At last the cartoon on the front cover makes sense!) This did not prove over productive and we disbanded after three years. Although we kept well in touch, there was a very strong bond between us and we had not met for many years until the Spring of 2007 when we met at a hotel somewhere mid was between Hoylake and Malvern. It was a wonderful day out but it was also obvious that Bert was not very well. Arrangements were made for us to go to Malvern about a month later, but his wife persuaded us not to go as he was very weak and a few weeks later I received the sad news that he had died. But he has never really died within me and I always will give thanks for a wonderful friendship punctuated at times in our naval years with a number of hair raising experiences, in addition to war ones, and I feel the loss greatly even though in recent years we saw so little of each other Before leaving Bert I would just add a happy reminder of him We were attending a church service in Portsmouth for ex MTB officers and crews, the service was conducted by the then Chaplain of the Fleet who related this story to us whilst giving his sermon. He had been the chief guest at some Naval Dinner and was being introduced by a retired Rear Admiral who regaled the audience at great length about the Japanese Naval hostilitics and in particular the "Kamikaze" Pilots. He then explained he had brought in the word "Kamikaze" which translates as "Divine Wind", and finished with the words "What better way was there to introduce the Chaplain of the Fleet!

In the Autumn of 2007 we had booked a cruise on the Queen Elizabeth 2, this being one of her final trips before retirement after forty years of travelling the oceans of the world. I was very interested to see how the journey and facilities would differ from my three cruises on the Saga

Rose. It certainly was different, firstly the size and the general arrangements, the casino and the fruit machines! But it was a very pleasant trip through the Mediterranean reaching as far as Alexandria. The day trip to the pyramids was both tiring and disappointing, perhaps because it was so restless and perhaps because we had seen them so many times on films (without the smells). On the whole I was a little disappointed more so because we had a most disgusting dirty bathroom which brought no response when I complained, except that I was sent a Voucher for £400 off any future trip! The other disappointment was that some of its internal grandeur had been removed to make more room for accommodation, which was a tribute to the modern world of greedy commerce by the American owners. I nevertheless would not have missed the experience of being aboard such a famous Queen of the Seas.

To bring this journey through my life up to date I would like to finish on a very special note. Whilst in the last chapter I related about my service on the Statutory Committee there is one closing incident which I feel is appropriate to record at this point. I had mentioned previously that the present and past members had been meeting once a year and as great changes are taking place within the Society this was an occasion for a final and appropriate meeting. The Government have decreed that the Regulatory Function is to be removed to a General Pharmaceutical Council (devised by this Governments insatiable desire to protect the public) and so as this meeting was to be the last one, the now retiring Chairman Lord Peter Fraser of Carmyllie invited us to dine with him at the House of Lords. This was a very great honour and some sixteen of us, including our ladies, sat down to dine in the close proximity of the famous and well known. This was a fitting end to a Committee that had seen many important members serving on it since 1932 and I felt very proud and honoured to have been one of this illustrious company.

EPILOGUE

*How many roads must a man walk down before he becomes man?
The answer my friend is blowing in the wind – the answer is blowing in the wind.*

Many years ago I made a very cynical remark to the effect that educating too many people would end in disaster. To this extent I have been proved partially correct in that over the years everyone seems to have become an expert! In my early days there was much more contentment and calm than in the frustrated "I know better" world that pertains today, so perhaps I should amend this and say that education has brought about great changes, but not all for the better. The most significant change has been the advance of Socialism which has benefited more than it has disappointed, but I still ask why the left wing element is dominated and ruled by leaders from the professions and upper classes, which they always hated. Which also brings to mind the total change in moral values, the arrogance in the financial world and the total disbelief in Members of Parliament especially for their "pigs in the trough" behaviour, and their apparent contempt for others.

I have in my narrative attempted to enlighten the reader of the various facets of life in this country which have passed my way. I cite the enormous changes in the Health Service, not all for the best, and the rise in bureaucracy in that service which at times seems to overlook the fact that their main objectives are to attend to the needs of patients. It has not all been negative and my experiences of bargaining with the various unions convinces me they do more good than is realised though some of this forward thinking gets lost when they return to the old "hate the rich" doctrine, when things do not go their way. I am very mindful that I may have appeared to neglect the other side of life, my children and their children but rather this narrative tries to explain to them mysteries they may have pondered about. It would appear that I feel a little concious about this but in reality I can look on so many happy times I have had with John and Peter and the joy I have experienced as they have progressed in to their own adulthood and their onward progress in life.

As I write this now nearing my 90th Birthday I am rather disappointed to find after all these years that greed and envy have increased, as better conditions seem to have produced a more selfish outlook on life and attempts to correct this do not meet with much success, and in my case I usually am criticised for looking back too often. Sometimes it is necessary to look back in order to face the future! As for the future, I of course cannot predict, but for some time my mind has been occupied with the thought that perhaps we are starting to witness the end of the Western Civilisation as we know it. My thoughts are simply my noting the demise of other civilisations like the Roman Empire, the Chinese Empire and the era of the Pharaohs. Of course I do not expect this to happen just yet, but I do feel the first signs are showing. Finally I have had a good innings (and there is still more to come), have seen many changes, been through a global War, but much more important, I have made many good friends, and I know in my heart that there are many more good people in this world than bad ones. Now I simply need to find something to bring this narrative to a close,and what better can there be than a little humility! So here goes!

Sometime when you're feeling important
Sometime when your ego's in bloom
Sometime when you're taken for granted
you're the best one in the room

Sometime when you feel that your going
Would leave an unfillable hole just follow
these simple instructions
And see how they humble your soul

Take a bucket and fill it with water
Put your hands in it up to your wrists
Pull them out, and the hole that remains
Is the measure that you will be missed

You may stir all you please when you enter
You may splash up the water galore
But stop __ and you'll find in a minute
That it looks just the same as before

The Moral of this is quite simple
Do just the best that you can
Be proud of yourself, but remember
"There is no indispensable man"

CURRICULUM VITAE

Geoffrey Stafford Knowles
Seaways Cottage
Marine Road
Hoylake

Born December 10th 1919

Educated at The King's School, Chester
Qualified as a Pharmacist from Liverpool School of Pharmacy
Commissioned in the Royal Navy 1943 serving on MTB's and Minesweepers
Proprietor of three pharmacies in Wirral 1948-1983

Appointed Justice of the Peace 1970
Designated as a Fellow of the Royal Pharmaceutical Society 1971
Vice President and Fellow of the Institute of Pharmacy Management
Fellow of the Australian Institute of Pharmacy Management
Founder member of the College of Pharmacy Practice

Life Member of both Royal Mersey Yacht Club and Hoylake Sailing Club

Health Service:
Member and Secretary of Cheshire Pharmaceutical Committee 1951-1974
Member Cheshire Executive Council 1965-1974
Member of Joint Prescription Pricing Committee for England 1971-1974
Member Cheshire Advisory Committee on Drug Abuse 1970-1974

On Reorganisation of Health Services 1974:

Member and Vice Chairman Wirral Area Health Authority 1974-82 followed by Wirral District Health Authority 1982-87

Member National Whitley Council (Admin and Clerical)

Member and Vice Chairman Prescription Pricing Authority 1974-89

Member Mersey Regional Nurse Training Committee 1978-82

Member Wirral Family Practitioner Committee 1974-82

Hon. Member and Finance Adviser to Wirral Postgraduate Medical Centre

Chairman Hoylake Cottage Hospital Trust 1985-88 and continuing until 2007

Appointed Member of the Statutory Committee of the Royal Pharmaceutical Society 1089-95

Appointed Honorary Auditor the Royal Pharmaceutical Society 1994-96

Letters

I especially have been grateful to you for your support when you were Vice Chairman of the Authority and I am very happy that now you will be taking on the responsibility for the Hoylake Cottage Hospital Trust. The loss to the Health Authority is to the gain of this organisation.

Phyllis Roberts
Chairman, Wirral Health Authority

I write on behalf of the Secretary of State to thank you for your much valued contribution to the work of the Prescription Pricing Authority, including, of course, your service as Vice-Chairman of the Authority. There have been many changes in the way the Authority carried out its responsibilities during your term of office, all have which benefited from your advice.

K. J. Guinness
Department of Health, London

At the last meeting of the Authority, the Chairman and members expressed their gratitude for the work you have done as a member over a period of 18 years I would like to take this opportunity of expressing my personal appreciation of your support and commitment, particularly in the critical field of industrial relations and staff side negotiations.

Alan Hilton, Chief Executive
The Prescription Pricing Authority

I write to offer my congratulations on your appointment to the Statutory Committee of the Royal Pharmaceutical Society. As one of the Officers of the Society I can tell you we had little hesitation when your name was proposed. There was unanimous approval of this and of course, Council were supportive of this nomination. It is in my opinion a most prestigious appointment in which the profession is expressing confidence in your balanced judgement.

Prof. T. G. Booth
University of Bradford

Speaking personally, and I think I speak for the rest of the Committee, I have always felt greatly reassured if Geoffrey is reassured because he is not somebody you can bowl many fast balls past without him noticing, and if he feels happy about something I feel enormously reassured

Gary Flather QC
Chairman of the Statutory Committee

Following the re-opening of Hoylake Cottage Hospital after closure, Geoffrey was the first Chairman 1985-1988. He worked tirelessly in his commitment and support of the ethos of the "Community Hospital". Geoffrey's contribution will remain an integral part of the annals of Hoylake Cottage Hospital's history.

Michael Taylor
Chairman Hoylake Cottage Hospital

Geoffrey's service has been tireless, continuous and invaluable. He brings real dedication and enthusiasm, which combined with his accountancy and political skills, has made possible much of the progress we have made over the years. His skill, wise counsel and dedication have guided our governing bodies through difficult and complex times despite many reorganisations inherent in NHS matters.

Dr W. R. Bell LDS
Chairman Wirral Postgraduate Medical Centre